Choral Counting & Counting Collections

Transforming the PreK–5 Math Classroom

Megan L. Franke, Elham Kazemi, and
Angela Chan Turrou

Stenhouse Publishers
Portsmouth, New Hampshire

Stenhouse Publishers
www.stenhouse.com

Library of Congress Cataloging-in-Publication Data
Names: Franke, Megan L., 1960– | Kazemi, Elham, 1970– | Turrou,
    Angela Chan, 1981–
Title: Choral Counting and Counting Collections : transforming the preK–5
    math classroom / [edited by] Megan L. Franke, Elham Kazemi, and Angela
    Chan Turrou.
Description: Portsmouth, New Hampshire: Stenhouse Publishers, [2018] |
    Includes index. Identifiers: LCCN 2018004788 (print) | LCCN 2018013506
    (ebook) | ISBN 9781625311108 (ebook) | ISBN 9781625311092 (pbk. : alk.
    paper)
Subjects: LCSH: Mathematics—Study and teaching (Elementary)—Activity
    programs. | Counting. | Mathematical recreations. | Communication in
    education.
Classification: LCC QA135.6 (ebook) | LCC QA135.6 .C5284 2018 (print) |
    DDC 372.7/2—dc23
LC record available at https://lccn.loc.gov/2018004788

Cover design, interior design, and typesetting by Martha Drury
Manufactured in the United States of America
Cover photo courtesy of Julie Kern Schwerdtfeger

PRINTED ON 30% PCW
RECYCLED PAPER

23 22 21 20 19   9 8 7 6 5 4 3

For William and Grace Chan
Abolghassem and Nahid Kazemi
Paul and Constance Loef

Contents

Acknowledgments

This book grew out of our collaborations across many communities to explore and experiment with the rich mathematics that can emerge from counting together with learners of many ages. It would not be possible without the creativity and passions of teachers, students, young children, and families. Thank you for sharing your ideas with us so we could share them with the world. Many teachers experimented with these activities and provided us with vivid ways to enact Choral Counting and Counting Collections in the classroom.

We are thankful to learn with and from the mathematics coaches and teachers in the Lawndale Elementary School District who continue to center counting in their practice with both children and their families. We would like to acknowledge the teachers at UCLA Lab School who bring Counting Collections to life across the grades and who are devoted to sharing their practices with others, with special thanks to Kim Morchower, Andrea Phillips, and Rosángela Viera for many of the examples we provide of Counting Collections in the upper grades. We are also grateful for the editorial expertise and support provided by Laura Weishaupt at UCLA Lab School.

Teachers at Lakeridge and Bryn Mawr Elementary Schools inspired examples across the Choral Counting and Counting Collections chapters at all grade levels. Thanks especially to Patti LaTurner for her never-ending excitement about her students and our work together. Savannah Menard's class gave us many ideas for Counting Collections in the primary grades. We appreciate Theresa Tse for sharing her experience and knowledge of Choral Counting. For their thoughtful contributions to Choral Counting in the primary grades, we would like to acknowledge Belvedere Elementary School teachers Allyson Gray and Steve Miner and Driscoll K–8 School teacher Jenna Laib. A special thanks to our preschool colleagues, Nidia Muñiz, Ana L. Rosales, Faviola Salcedo, Dolores Torres, and Guadalupe Villalpando, for sharing their classrooms and expertise with us. We are inspired by the growing number of educators, such as Ms. Shala, who are including families in their mathematics education efforts.

No project can ever come to fruition without the support of our friends and families who supported our constant search for and storage of Counting Collections, allowed us to try our next choral count, and gave us time and space for quiet writing time. We are indebted to Toby Gordon, our editor, whose encouragement, keen editing eye, and patience allowed us to make this book a reality.

Contributors

Darlene Fish Doto is currently a third- and fourth-grade educator at San Carlos Charter Learning Center. She was formerly Lead Demonstration Teacher in Mathematics at UCLA Lab School.

Megan L. Franke is a professor of education in the Graduate School of Education and Information Studies at UCLA. She is coauthor of *Children's Mathematics: Cognitively Guided Instruction, Young Children's Mathematics: Cognitively Guided Instruction in Early Childhood Education,* and *Thinking Mathematically: Integrating Arithmetic and Algebra in Elementary School.*

Natali Gaxiola is a preschool teacher for the Lennox School District, where she has supported colleagues through coaching in the area of mathematics.

Lynsey Gibbons is an assistant professor of mathematics education at Boston University. She is interested in how to organize schools to support teachers' and students' ongoing learning.

Allison Hintz is an associate professor of mathematics education at the University of Washington Bothell. She is coauthor with Elham Kazemi of *Intentional Talk: How to Structure and Lead Productive Mathematical Discussions.*

Carolee Koehn Hurtado is an assistant professor of education at CSU Channel Islands and enjoys bringing teachers and families together to support children's mathematical thinking. She is coauthor of *Reimagining the Mathematics Classroom: Creating and Sustaining Productive Learning Environments, K–6.*

Nick Johnson is a postdoctoral scholar at UCLA. He studies children's mathematical thinking and is coauthor of *Young Children's Mathematics: Cognitively Guided Instruction in Early Childhood Education.*

Elham Kazemi is a professor of mathematics education at the University of Washington. She is interested in how teachers work together to learn from and with their students. She is coauthor with Allison Hintz of *Intentional Talk: How to Structure and Lead Productive Mathematical Discussions.*

Stephanie Latimer is a math coach at Bryn Mawr Elementary school in the Renton School District. As a math coach, she is interested in how to best support teacher practice and students' mathematical ideas with Choral Counting and Counting Collections.

Teresa Lind is a math coach at Lakeridge Elementary in the Renton School District. She supports teacher practice and student learning through math labs and embedded professional development.

Kendra Lomax is the managing director of Teacher Education by Design at the University of Washington. She designs and facilitates job-embedded professional learning opportunities for elementary teachers.

Brandon McMillan is a doctoral candidate at UCLA in the Graduate School of Education. He studies student mathematical thinking to connect elementary and middle school mathematics instruction. In addition, he facilitates workshops for teachers and families centered on students' thinking.

Julie Kern Schwerdtfeger is a demonstration teacher at UCLA Lab School. She also works with the UCLA Math Project to continue teaching and learning about children's mathematical thinking alongside her colleagues in the Los Angeles Unified School District.

Angela Chan Turrou is a senior researcher at UCLA. She is coauthor of *Young Children's Mathematics: Cognitively Guided Instruction in Early Childhood Education.*

Kassia Omohundro Wedekind is a math coach at Belvedere Elementary School in Fairfax County Public Schools. She is the author of *Math Exchanges: Guiding Young Mathematicians in Small-Group Meetings.*

CHAPTER 1

Introduction

by Megan L. Franke, Elham Kazemi, and
Angela Chan Turrou

Count Everything, Count All the Time!

This book is all about counting. Counting objects like pencils and beads and packages of crayons. Counting just a few seashells as you and your students move them carefully from one pile to another. Counting paper clips that come in boxes of 125 by first counting the 100s and then the 25s. Counting by 1s. Counting by 4s and 10s and 1200s. Counting by 5s but starting at 22 instead of zero. Counting all kinds of numbers, like fractions and decimals. Counting forward into the thousands. Counting backward (maybe even into the negatives!). This book is about the counting that you already do with your students and about counting in ways you have not yet imagined.

Counting Matters

Counting is fundamental to learning mathematics in elementary school. It supports the development of a deep understanding of number, providing the core foundation for understanding place value, how numbers are composed and decomposed, and how they are related to one another. This deep understanding of numbers allows students to operate on them in powerful ways. These days we are not just asking children to calculate answers to simple arithmetic problems digit by digit. We are asking them to try out and even invent sophisticated mathematical strategies that leverage number relationships and our base 10 number structure in complex ways, using algebraic ideas and the fundamental

1

properties—even in kindergarten. All this means that we need to push beyond the traditions of counting and skip-counting to 100 and of assuming that children just get what happens beyond 100. Children need ample and varied experiences with all kinds of numbers to support them in their mathematics sense making; they do this through counting.

Counting from a Child's Point of View

As adults, it is easy to take counting for granted. When presented with a reasonable quantity to count, we count efficiently and accurately in ways that leverage our strong sense of number and organizational skills. From a proficient counter's point of view, we often fail to appreciate that counting is an intricate process requiring the coordination of much skill and knowledge developed over time. Watching a child count, however, helps us to notice the complicated details of counting. We see a variety of things happen when we pose different kinds of counting tasks to children: children say their numbers and point to objects in ways that don't always match up, children count and recount the same object in a collection because it's hard to keep track, children count into the 20s and 30s but don't quite know which number comes after 49 ("What's it called again? Is it *five-ee*?"), children count by 10s but crossing 100 say, "101" or "200." Children who are learning to count in a new language may skip number words or pause more often. They may be more successful counting in their primary language. We don't see these as mistakes that we are trying to fix, but, rather, these common events illuminate the complex terrain of counting and remind us as educators that we need to continue to provide broad counting experiences throughout elementary school.

Introducing Counting Collections and Choral Counting

We focus on two particular activities for supporting the development of counting from preschool through elementary school: Counting Collections and Choral Counting (see Appendixes 1 and 2 for planning tools). We have chosen these activities for four main reasons. First, children like to participate in them, and they create opportunities for children with a range of skills and understandings to join in. Second, they are routines that teachers and students alike want to do often; each time students participate, they can bring new knowledge to the task and continue to improve their understanding. Third, the routine activities support students to make their thinking explicit and to do so with other students, the class, and the teacher. Fourth, these routine activities create continuity across classrooms and grades as well as provide an opportunity to connect from school to home to community. (See Figures 1.1 and 1.2.) We have seen teachers across a range of contexts use these activities in ways that support student participation and learning, and, in doing so, they have adapted, innovated, and made them their own (see Appendix 3 for video examples, readings, and blog posts depicting the activities in use in a range of grade levels and contexts).

Counting Collections and Choral Counting, while developing students' understanding of counting, offer different mathematical and participation opportunities. Counting Collections focuses in on *collections*, or groups of objects, in which students are asked to draw on the counting principles in relation to one another as they figure out how many objects they have. As they count objects, their varied ways of grouping and sorting enrich their understanding of counting. Choral Counting supports students to count together as the teacher records the number sequence in a specific manner. As they do so, students examine number relationships that enable them to identify, to discuss, and to use patterns and the structure of the number system. In Counting Collections, students have the opportunity to figure out how to count with a

Figure 1.1
A pair of students organize and count their collection.

Figure 1.2
A class shares patterns they notice when counting by 1s starting at 73.

partner or partners; they get to navigate mathematics, their explanations, and others' ideas as they figure out how to work together. In Choral Counting, students support one another often in the whole-group setting to count, to see relationships and patterns, to build on someone else's idea, and to ask different kinds of questions of the mathematics.

Using the same routine activities across classrooms and grades, in school and out, provides collaborative opportunities. Teachers can collaborate within a grade level to plan their choral count or how they want to structure their collections. After they have enacted their counting activities, they can chat informally or formally about what they learned about student thinking and what they might want to pursue next. Students can collaborate with one another inside the class or even, as we have seen in classrooms, count with students in another grade (for example, first graders can count with their third-grade buddies). Teachers can collaborate with families. We have seen teachers and families share the different ways counting happens in school and at home (and families often share collections of items they find at home with classrooms). The collaboration that occurs among teachers, students, and families supports common understandings of what it means to do math, to develop young mathematicians, and to build and generate new excitement with these activities.

These activities support students' participation and their mathematics identities.

We love these two activities for the space they provide for students to participate in varied ways as they cultivate a joy for mathematics and develop strong identities as doers of mathematics. While teachers may choose to implement and innovate these activities in varied ways, their core structures allow important mathematical interactions to occur in the classroom. Teachers elicit a variety of student contributions and use student ideas as the launch pad for further discussion. They orient students toward the ideas of their peers and often highlight ideas they did not consider themselves or ones they don't agree with or have questions about. Teachers ask follow-up questions that leverage the big mathematical ideas embedded within children's thinking and move the group toward important mathematical goals. Most important, as teachers and students engage with each other during these activities, student ideas are at the center, and these ideas drive the group's exploration of mathematics.

These activities support teachers to listen to and learn more about children's mathematical thinking.

What makes mathematics teaching so wonderful is that children are continually surprising us when we take the time to listen to their ideas. Because these activities create space for children to share their unique ways of thinking mathematically, you'll find yourself exploring all kinds of ideas with children in ways that connect to what intrigues them. The more you work these activities into the routine of your classroom practice, the more opportunities you'll have to learn about the details of children's thinking and make purposeful instructional decisions to build on these details.

These activities help us enact our commitments to equity.

We know that a sense of belonging and investment, of being seen, known, and heard by teachers and classmates, is fundamental to creating schools where children and families feel welcome and where they flourish. Because these activities foreground student sense making and cultivate a joy for doing mathematics, they can be powerful tools for teachers to counter narrow views that only a few can identify with mathematics or that mathematics is disconnected from students' home lives, their communities, and their own interests.

As teachers and teacher educators we recognize that engagement with Counting Collections and Choral Counting is shaped by the contexts of our schools and communities as well as the experiences, histories, and cultural practices of our students. The examples of young people and teachers engaged in Counting Collections and Choral Counting in this book are drawn from classrooms across the United States. Some are bilingual Spanish settings where students have the opportunity to learn mathematics in both Spanish and English, while in others many languages are spoken but the primary language of instruction is English. Some are in highly impacted urban communities and others in more rural communities, each serving families who have been historically marginalized. Some are in schools that predominately serve low-income students and others are schools that draw mixed-income populations. We encourage you to consider your school context, the community assets, and your students' cultural and linguistic resources as you think about how your students and families would engage these activities and how you might negotiate their use together.

Overview of the Activities

Counting Collections Overview

"Today, you and your partner and going to count a collection, figure out how many you have in your collection, and show me a picture of how you counted in your journal." These deceptively straightforward directions set children off to work on Counting Collections. Ms. Ho's kindergarteners are pushing to count past 109. Jenai and Samuel wonder what "one hundred twelve" looks like. Marcus and Jamie want to try counting their collection of buttons by 20s. Mr. Shahan's fifth graders have just been challenged to count all the panes in their window-filled classroom. They notice how the panes are arranged in arrays except in a few spots where a design is embedded in the windows. Mr. Shahan has suggested they negotiate and come up with a plan before they start, and he presses them to figure out a way to count the panes without counting by 1s. Students in both classrooms are eager to test their own ideas and are looking forward to sharing what they have figured out when their teachers come by to check on their progress.

In Counting Collections, children figure out how many items are in a collection of objects. (See Figures 1.3 and 1.4.) As they do so, they make a recording of their count. It is a powerfully simple idea, with multiple entry points for children's learning that is enduringly engaging and productive for learning in children of all ages. Collections vary in quantity and comprise a variety of items that are interesting for students to count and easily collect: shells, rocks, craft sticks, beads, dried pasta, marker tops, buttons, small toys, and so on. Collections can also consist of packaged items, such as packs of playing cards, packs of markers, boxes of paper clips, and sheets of stickers. (You'll find yourself looking at junk drawers, classroom supplies, dollar stores, and garage sales in a whole new light!)

Children make decisions about how to organize their collections, whether they want to use plates or cups or other aids such as ten-frames or hundred charts to help them organize their count. They count their collections by 1s or group objects to help them count. Children might work alone, but often they collaborate with a partner to count their collection. This pair work is a vital

Figure 1.3
Examples of collections of loose items.

Figure 1.4
Examples of packaged collections.

mechanism for learning to orient to someone else's idea because partners share ideas with one another, negotiate, sometimes restart, and problem-solve as they encounter challenges in how to count their collection and record their count. (See Appendix 1 for a range of recording sheets teachers have used.)

Let's drop into a first-grade classroom and listen to what children are saying as they figure out how to count their collections together. In this classroom, pairs of children have just chosen a collection, grabbed a pencil and a recording sheet, and found space within the classroom to work (some on the rug, some at the tables). They are busy pouring their collections out of the bag carefully so that they don't spill everywhere and discussing whether they want some organizing tools and which ones (e.g., little paper cups, paper bowls, nacho trays, egg cartons). As we look around, we see collections of different items and different quantities—a collection of clothespins in the 20s, a few dozen colored pencils, some bottle caps that might total more than 100. As we listen into students' conversations, we get a sense of the range of issues they are navigating as they count together:

"I got 10. How many you got?"
"Let's count by 2s. You move them, and I'll say the numbers."
"You count one, and then I'll count one. Let's make a line." "Okay. Let's put the line over here."
"I want to count by 4s." "But I don't know how to count by 4s." "Well, you put them in the cups, and I'll help with the numbers."
"27, 28, 29 . . ." (*pause*) Friend pipes in, "30! . . . 37, 38, 39 . . ." (*pause*) Friend pipes in, "40."
"How do you write twelve?" "1 and then a 2. Like this."

A critical feature of Counting Collections is that children make these decisions themselves. As we observe the buzz of activity of children engaging in varied ways with their collections, we notice that children's ideas remain at the center. It can be tempting for teachers to step in and direct how children should best count the collection, but important mathematical work is done as children coordinate their methods for counting with the way they organize the collection and how they choose to record the number of objects they have.

As children count their collections, the teacher circulates the room to watch and listen to their counting. The teacher confers with students to learn about their conceptions of quantities and how they use the counting principles. They will observe how students relate objects they're counting to their diagrams and pay attention to how they used notation. These intimate conversations help the teacher learn about and press children's thinking. "Can you recount your collection, counting a new way this time? Can you combine your groups of 10 and count your collection by a different amount? What tool in the room can you use to figure out how to write *131*?"

In a third-grade classroom, Ms. Jackson decides to check in with Pablo who was finished counting but seemed to be struggling with representing his count on paper. Pablo had been working with a partner (who had since gone to the bathroom) to count a collection of more than 400 craft beads. Ms. Jackson sees that they are organized in some small cups and wants to find out more from Pablo.

Ms. Jackson: It looks like you're done counting your collection. Can you tell me what you did?

Pablo: Cameron and I counted 425 beads.

Ms. Jackson: Wow, 425 sounds like a lot. How did you and Cameron count?

Pablo: Well, we wanted to do 10 in a cup, but the cups were filling up the whole table and starting to fall off the table; so I said we needed to put the cups together or we would run out of room.

Ms. Jackson: I see. So how did you put the cups together?

Pablo: First, we did two 10s and that made 20. But then we heard Julissa and Elijah over there counting by 25, and so we wanted to count by 25. So, we put 5 more into the cup and made 25 in a cup.

Ms. Jackson: Oh, so there's 25 in each of these cups?

Pablo: Yeah. All of them had 25. It fit with no leftovers.

Ms. Jackson: No leftovers? Wow. Then it looks like you stacked the cups. What were you doing there?

Pablo: Well, Cameron said he wanted to do 50 and 50 is 100, so we stacked the cups because 25 and 25 is 50 and 50 and 50 is 100. So then we counted one, two, three, four 100s, and then one cup is 425. But now I don't know what I should write down.

Ms. Jackson: Hmm, where do you think you could start?

Pablo: I don't know. Maybe I could put 100s?

Ms. Jackson: Yes, I think the 100s is a great idea. How could you show the 100s?

Pablo: Well, we put the cups together to count by 100s.

Ms. Jackson: Could you show how you put the cups together to make the 100s?

Pablo: Hmm, maybe like this?

(Ms. Jackson looks over Pablo's shoulder as he begins to draw his stacked cups of 25s and indicates how he grouped the 25s into 100.) (See Figure 1.5.)

Figure 1.5
Pablo's representation of 25s.

Through interactions with students, the teacher can also provide support for children's counting and recordings and for working together productively. Because the teacher pays close attention to what children are trying, thinking, and doing, she leads conversations with the whole class that can take place at the beginning and at the end of the activity. She might highlight how particular students have been strategically using new organizing tools over the past few days or the ways in which students are deciding together how they plan to keep track of what they have already counted and what they still need to count.

In the chapters that lie ahead, you will see many different examples of how and when teachers have chosen to launch or close Counting Collections with a whole-group conversation. These conversations can help spread new ideas throughout the room, highlight new insights children are gaining from Counting Collections, and give children new challenges to consider in their counting work.

Counting Collections is a rich activity that creates an ever-evolving range of social and mathematical learning opportunities that change based on a variety of factors:

- how big the collection is (28 hair clips vs. 241 stickers vs. more than 1,000 beans)
- how the children decide to organize their collection (counting one by one vs. organizing into groups of 5 vs. creating an array with rows of 10)
- if the collection comes in "individual" versus "packaged" items (loose crayons vs. crayons in packages of 4; loose paper clips vs. packages of 125 or 200)
- how students navigate the social and mathematical demands of the task (deciding on a strategy to use, how to count, whether to count together, keeping track of which items have been counted and which have not, etc.)
- how the teacher chooses to interact with children to understand and extend their thinking (asking students to organize their collection in a different way, encouraging students to try a different strategy when theirs is not working, prompting students to consider how many more they would need to reach 100, asking students to represent their collection using symbolic notation, etc.)

Critical Features of Counting Collections
• Children count a collection of objects, typically but not always with a partner
• Children choose how to count the collection, including how to use space, whether to use tools, how to organize their collection, how to work together to count
• Teachers may choose type of collection (quantities, kinds of objects) and which children to pair for both academic and social goals
• During or after counting, children choose how to make a recording of their count to show how and what they counted
• While children count, the teacher circulates the classroom to confer with children, listen to them count, have instructional conversations to understand students' strategies, and when appropriate, press their thinking
• Before, during or after the count teachers may choose to highlight insights children are developing

Choral Counting Overview

"Let's push ourselves with today's count. Today, we're going to count by 15. I'm going to give you a moment to think about what that might sound like. Are we ready?" Ms. Lawyer's students *chorally count* from 15 together with support from the teacher while she writes the numbers on the board neatly in a column of 6. Ms. Lawyer pauses the count at 90 and asks students how they figured out that 90 came after 75. She elicits a few ideas from the group: Audrey likes to add 10 and then 5; Sean thinks about the 5 first, then the 10; Vilma is beginning to see jumps of 30 as you skip a number. Ms. Lawyer checks in with the group to make sure everyone has his or her own way to keep going and then supports the group to continue the count together. At times, the students quiet down and stumble a bit (such as when they approach the 200s); other times, they excitedly grow loud (such as when the count "starts over" at 300, and they can use what they had already counted at the beginning).

When the group gets to 390, Ms. Lawyer asks students to stop and take a moment to look at the entire, organized number sequence. She prompts them by asking, "What do you notice about the numbers? Turn to a partner and share one thing you noticed."

Ms. Lawyer and her class are engaged in one of their favorite counting activities: Choral Counting. This is an activity they have engaged in regularly throughout the year, one that is met with much excitement, math chitchat, and eager students bursting to share their noticings.

In this whole-group activity, the teacher supports the students to chorally count together as the teacher publicly records, in a preplanned organized manner, the numbers they have counted. The teacher chooses a starting number, which number to count by, and how she wants to represent the count. The count could be counting by 1s, a classic skip-count (counting by 2, 5, 20, 20, etc.), a count starting at a number other than 0 or 1 (counting by 4 starting at 180, counting by 2 starting at 1, etc.), a fraction/decimal count (count by $\frac{1}{4}$, $\frac{7}{8}$, etc.), a backward count (count backward by 20, starting at 400, etc.), and the list continues. The count could be organized in rows or columns of differing quantities, with different representations highlighting different number relationships. Ms. Lawyer played around with different representations using the *Choral Counting Planning Tool** (see sten.pub/choralcounting) before she chose her organization in columns of 6 (see Appendix 2 for the *Choral Counting Planning Template*).

The teacher then makes a range of planned and in-the-moment decisions to support students to count together. She may elicit student strategies (just as Ms. Lawyer did), pause before an anticipated bump in the count (e.g., before crossing the 100 or the 1,000 mark), back up a couple of rows or columns and have the group recount to reestablish the rhythmic cadence, prompt students to figure out an upcoming number with a partner, and so on. The goal is to support the group to count together, knowing that a range of student participation is likely to occur and students may engage with the count differently.

After the students count together (far enough to get a good chunk of numbers on the board), the teacher launches a purposeful conversation about the number sequence that is up on the board, often with the open and inviting question, *What do you notice?* The goal of this question is to get students to engage with the organized number sequence in ways that make sense to them and provide multiple entry points for a range of responses to be a valued contribution to the conversation. Let's look at Ms. Lawyer's count (see Figure 1.6). Ms. Lawyer invited students to think about what they notice in the numbers and then prompted a partner share to discuss these ideas. These are some examples of what Ms. Lawyer's students noticed and shared during this count; as she elicited student ideas, she recorded them publicly by marking up the number sequence.

- It alternates 5, 0, 5, 0 in the ones place.
- Skipping a number is just like counting by 30.

---

*We designed an online tool to help you play around with how you want to write the count. The tool allows you to input what you want to count by and where you want to start. You can see how the count will look if the numbers go across a row or down a column. Perhaps you want to see what a count looks like with fractions or with decimals. What would a backward count look like? Input these parameters, and you'll be able to print out and compare different possibilities in recording the count.

- The bottom row is just counting by 90—we're adding 90.
- Going up the diagonal, we are adding 75.
- There are 7 numbers in the 100s, 6 in the 200s, 7 in the 300s, so I wonder how many are going to be in the 400s.
- Going across the row, the digit in the tens place decreases by 1 (in the bottom row, 9, 8, 7, 6 . . .).
- It goes 10, 30, 40, 60, 70, . . . so it seems like we skip some of the tens but not all of them.

You can see from the spread of ideas here (Figure 1.6) that the goal is to support a range of students to participate. No matter the ease or difficulty of the count, each student can notice something and contribute to the conversation. This is a critical feature of this task, inviting a range of student participation and supporting each student to contribute. We have conducted this activity in many classrooms and shared this activity with teachers over the years. Teachers consistently report that Choral Counting, in particular, often elicits sharing from students who ordinarily hesitate to speak up in math. Making Choral Counting part of the classroom routine helps students see themselves as capable mathematicians, as valued doers of math, who have an important role to play within the mathematics classroom.

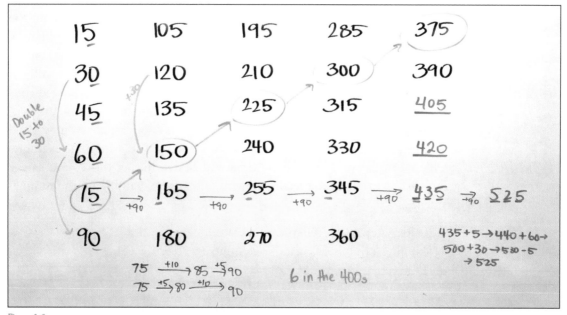

Figure 1.6
Choral Counting by 15 with annotations marking patterns.

Orienting Students Toward Their Peers' Ideas

Teachers can work to build community around counting and noticing by asking other students to engage with the shared ideas. A teacher may simply ask, "Did anyone else notice what Amiah saw down the column?" or "Amiah noticed the bottom row is adding 90. Do you see that happening in any other row?" Often it can be interesting to ask students to predict an upcoming number that can be figured out using an idea just shared; we can use Amiah's idea to predict what will come directly to the right of the 345. In listening to the ideas of others, students often note new things they could do or add to the conversation. In hearing Amiah's idea about the 90s, Marcus says, "I can make 90s going down, too."

Asking Follow-Up Questions

When students share their own ideas, the teacher may wish to ask a follow-up question that prompts for clarification, presses for more detail, or builds on the idea being shared. It can be particularly interesting to follow up on a student noticing with a "why?" question, such as, "Why do you think Ernesto's pattern works? Why does it increase by 75 as you move up the diagonal?" Such questions invite students to dive into the mathematical ideas underlying what students notice. Here is where the teacher can really leverage student contributions to move toward particular mathematical goals.

Let's jump back into another classroom: this time into Ms. Lockhart's first grade and listen in on the kinds of conversations that occur as students share their ideas and the teacher finds ways to orient students to each other's ideas and ask follow-up questions. (See Figure 1.7.)

Figure 1.7
Choral Counting
by 5.

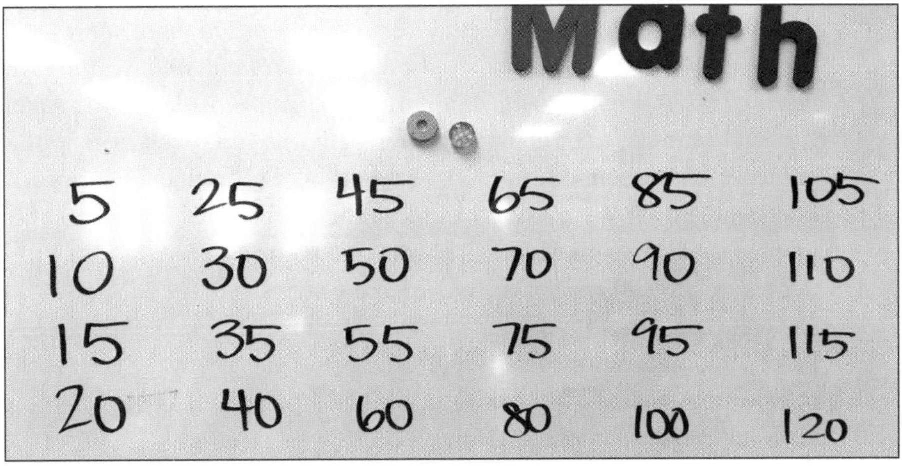

5	25	45	65	85	105
10	30	50	70	90	110
15	35	55	75	95	115
20	40	60	80	100	120

Ms. Lockhart: Who wants to share something they noticed? (*pause*) Zayan?

Zayan: I see something in the tens!

Ms. Lockhart: Tell me where you see something in the tens.

Zayan: There, in the second row. The tens go 1, 3, 5, 7, 9.

    (*Ms. Lockhart marks the tens digit across the numbers in the second row.*)

Ms. Lockhart: Great, thank you, Zayan. Who else wants to share? (*pause*) Elli, what did you notice?

Elli, (*pointing to the bottom left corner of the representation and gesturing across*)**:** It's counting by 20 there (*increasing by 20s across the column*)!

Ms. Lockhart: Elli says it's counting by 20. Does everyone else see the counting by 20? (*students hesitant, murmuring*) Elli, could you say more about that? Where do you see it?

Elli, (*pointing again*)**:** There!

Ms. Lockhart: Which numbers are you looking at?

Elli: The 20! And 40, 60, 80 . . .

Ms. Lockhart, (*underlines the numbers that Elli is referring to*)**:** Do we all see where Elli says it's counting by 20s? (*more agreement*) Elli, can you count them again, and we'll count with you? 20 . . . (*class counts the bottom row together as the teacher gestures to each number: 20, 40, 60, 80, 100, 120, . . .*)

Ms. Lockhart: All right, nice counting. I have a question though. Today's count is counting by 5s, but Elli noticed we're counting by 20s in the bottom row. Why do you think we're counting by 20s here: 20, 40, 60, 80 . . . ? (*pause*) Turn and talk to a partner about what you're thinking.

Critical Features of Choral Counting

- Publicly record the number sequence in a preplanned, organized manner
- Support students to count together (e.g., *Who wants to share how they figured out it would be _____? Let's back up to the top of this column and recount together. Let's pause here and take a moment with your partner to figure out what comes next.*)
- Count far enough to be able to notice repetitions and regularities in the number sequence (and where the regularities might hold for awhile then break)
- Invite students to share a range of ideas about what they notice about the numbers (allow for multiple points of entry into discussion)
- Represent student ideas in the recorded number sequence
- Facilitate conversation by leveraging student ideas and making a range of follow-up moves: asking for more detail, supporting students to engage with each other's ideas, pressing for explanation/justification when appropriate, digging into big mathematical ideas underlying student noticings

In this example, Ms. Lockhart is leveraging student ideas and making purposeful decisions about when and how to follow up and in what way. As with any mathematical activity that uses student ideas as the foundation, the teacher is always delicately navigating a range of social and mathematical goals while staying true to letting students and their ideas be the drivers of the conversation. This is not an easy task but one in which teachers get ample practice as they find that Choral Counting is a task they revisit frequently, both because they see the mathematical value of students' deepening understanding of number and because students practically demand it.

The Content of Counting

Counting is a mathematical domain we often consider the responsibility of preschool and kindergarten. However, learning to count occurs over the course of years and serves as the foundation for understanding much of the mathematical work we do in elementary school. Counting involves pattern, structure, quantity, and number sense and can be extended to involve grouping, multiplicative reasoning, fractions, and decimals.

Learning to count is often seen as learning the number sequence—knowing that we count 1, 2, 3, 4 or 98, 99, 100, 101. The counting sequence follows a pattern that represents the structure that underlies our number system. We see that pattern at play when children count 37, 38, 39 and then say, 10, 20, 30, 40 to see that 40 will come next. We see it when children count 119, 120 or 999, 1,000. We also see it when children struggle to remember the sequence in the teens where the number words do not make the structure explicit as students try and remember that 12 (not *ten two*) comes after 11 (*ten one*). Learning the number sequence means more than learning to memorize the number names; it involves raising out the

structure that underlies the sequence to help children see the patterns and understand how those patterns enable them to efficiently and elegantly use the number system. Counting Collections and Choral Counting support children to work on making the structure of the number sequence explicit.

Learning the counting sequence is one important piece of learning to count, but it is only one piece. Children also need to learn about the other counting principles. The counting principles include the one-to-one principle (most often referred to as one-to-one correspondence) and the cardinal principle.

Counting principles:
There is an **ordered sequence of counting numbers,** and numbers are always assigned to items in a collection in the same order starting with 1.
The one-to-one principle. Exactly one number from the counting sequence is assigned to each item in the collection.
The cardinal principle. The last number in the counting sequence assigned to the collection represents the number of objects in the collection.

To count a collection of objects, a sequence of events, a collection of noises, and so on, children need to coordinate all of the counting principles. Children do not need to know the counting principles prior to counting a collection; they develop their understanding of the principles *while* they count collections. You will see throughout the counting collection work that teachers regularly ask students, *How many in your collection?* That question focuses on cardinality. The response requires that children know that the last number they said in the counting sequence is the total number in their collection. Children do not need to know the cardinal principle to count a collection; if they don't, they will recount, tell you a random number, or say they don't know. But this provides the opportunity to work on the principle.

Students do not learn the counting principles in a set order. Some children will learn a piece of the counting sequence before developing understanding of one-to-one correspondence, while others will have some understating of one-to-one correspondence and not yet know the counting sequence. This becomes important as children work on Counting Collections. In school, we often ask children to count a collection of 3 until they have developed an understanding of the counting principles and then 4 and so on. It turns out that this is not necessary and limits students' abilities to draw on all they know to continue to learn the principles.

As children develop their understanding of the counting principles, they are also developing number sense. They are learning about the relationship between the numbers and the quantities. They see which numbers are larger than others, which are close to 10, which numbers are 1 less, 1 more, and so on. They also begin to develop a sense of quantity—what does 5 things look like, or how large is 50 in comparison to 5. As they continue to count, they begin to see other patterns in the 10s, in the 1s, across the 100s. All of these patterns support students' understanding of place value and operations.

One of the most central patterns in the number system for elementary school students is the relationship between 1s, 10s, 100s, 1000s and so on. We often teach this relationship in place value as identifying the "places." A focus on the places masks both the underlying relationship and how understanding the structure of the number system can help one mathematically. The conceptual underpinnings of the ones and tens places are that ten 1s make a 10, and this pattern continues so that ten 10s make a 100. Students can use their understanding of ten as a unit (understanding that ten 1s make up a 10) to help them solve problems. Counting Collections and Choral Counting each support the development of students place value understanding. In Counting Collections, students get to work on creating groups of ten 1s to make a 10 and then begin to use those 10s to count their entire collection; students' representations of their collections help them use and generalize patterns. When Choral Counting, students can work on how the counting sequence will continue after counting 73, 83, 93 or how counting by 11 is the same as counting one 10 and a 1 or when looking at patterns notice that 453 has forty-five 10s.

As students organize their collections or look for patterns in a choral count, they can also begin to build their ideas of grouping and multiplicative reasoning. Early on, young children will often group the items in the collection, especially if the collection varies by features such as colors, type of animal, size, and so on. They may not be able to use the groups to count the entire collection, but they can build, recognize, name, and tell the quantity of these groups. As students continue to count collections, they will group to help them with their counting—grouping objects regardless of feature into 2s, 5s, 10s, and so on. Now they are using groups to help them organize and potentially count the total amount in their collection. Students can then group within their groups. Here students may be counting a bucket of crayons and sort them by 10s and then realize in counting that they could count half of the groups and double them, writing on their paper $(6 \times 10) + (6 \times 10)$ or $(6 \times 10) \times 2$.

We often do not think about counting with fractions and decimals; yet, students need to the opportunity to develop the same deep understandings of quantity and number sense with fractions and decimals as they do with whole numbers. There is great power for students in understanding what they can do with a unit fraction such as $\frac{1}{3}$ or 0.10 or 0.01. Students can learn how these create a whole or how they are more or less than a whole. They can work on what it means to add, to subtract, to multiply, and to divide and what it means to do these operations when you have less than 1. When students then begin to work with non-unit fractions, they can use those understandings. Imagine what students notice when incrementing by $\frac{7}{8}$ in a choral count. They can think that $\frac{8}{8}$ is 1, so they are incrementing by $\frac{1}{8}$ less than 1, connecting their incrementing and $\frac{7}{8}$ to the whole. Or when incrementing decimals, students can see beyond how $\frac{10}{10}$ make 1 and see what happens when you continue to increment past one and go from 0.9 to 1.0 and 1.9 to 2.0 (often students think it goes 1.9, 1.10). In counting a collection, students can count objects seen as parts of a whole and begin to group them, which supports them to understand the multiplication of fractions as combining groups of $\frac{2}{3}$.

Overview of Chapters to Come

We have been using Choral Counting and Counting Collections in our classrooms and supporting teachers through our roles as university-based teacher educators or school-based mathematics coaches. We have adapted these activities for interactions with children in and out of school and in our roles as mathematics educators and parents.

One of the beautiful things about Counting Collections is that it is an activity you can do regularly in the classroom at any grade level across the year.

In Chapter 2, Allison Hintz and Stephanie Latimer help us see the joy of young mathematicians engaging in Counting Collections as they draw from their extensive work supporting teachers in school-based settings. In Chapter 3, Julie Kern Schwerdtfeger and Darlene Fish Doto give you a vision of the sophisticated territory that Counting Collections explores in the upper grades using examples from Julie's and others' classroom.

Just like Counting Collections, the beauty of Choral Counting is that it can be done in any grade level and on a frequent basis, while continuing to be productive for student learning and for student excitement in math. In Chapter 4, Lynsey Gibbons and Kassia Omohundro Wedekind help us see what Choral Counting can look like in the primary grades. Kendra Lomax and Teresa Lind take us into the upper grades in Chapter 5 to see how Choral Counting works with whole numbers, decimals, and fractions.

Chapter 6 brings us into the preschool setting, where Nick Johnson and Natali Gaxiola dive into the thinking of our youngest learners in Natali's preschool classroom. In Chapter 7, Carolee Koehn Hurtado and Brandon McMillan and then draw from their partnerships with schools and families to help us think about how to support connections outside of school.

Finally, Chapter 8 offers concluding thoughts about the power of coordinating the use of these activities for children, the connections to real-life counting, and advice from teachers about diving in and reveling in the messiness of getting started.

Note to Reader: While you may be tempted to read the chapters that are most targeted to your grade level, we encourage you to visit other chapters, as many ideas are applicable beyond the grade-level span in which they are described.

CHAPTER 2

Counting Collections K–2

by Allison Hintz and Stephanie Latimer

"19, 20, 21, 22, 23!" Deion and Astur exclaim as they point to each colorful popsicle stick lying in a row on the carpet. Deion pauses and stares at the row, and then he circles back to the first stick and begins counting aloud again. Astur joins in, "Yep, there's 23!" they both announce. (See Figure 2.1.)

Figure 2.1
Two boys counting
a row of 23 colorful
popsicle sticks.

"Okay, now let's draw it on our paper. How can we show how many are in our collection?" asks Deion. "We could draw a tally mark for each stick. Do you want to draw on our recording sheet or count?" replies Astur. "I'll draw, you count this time," says Deion as he begins drawing tally marks on their recording sheet. Astur points to each stick and counts aloud; he slows down as Deion works to keep up with drawing a mark for each number that is said.

They decide to write the total on the recording sheet, but neither student can remember what the symbol for twenty-three looks like. Looking up from their clipboard, they notice classmates huddled by the big hundreds chart on the wall and go over to hunt for their number. "There it is (pointing to 20, 21, 22, and landing on 23); it's two then three!" They scurry back to their clipboard and Astur writes *23*.

"Let's put this collection away and go get another one." Quickly walking off, you can hear, "Let's see if the collection of marbles is still there!"

Deion and Astur are Counting Collections in their kindergarten classroom. The pair sits among a sea of children spread around the classroom, all counting. A lively buzz fills the room as these young mathematicians make decisions about how to work together and how to find and record the total number of objects in their collections.

Watching these children so hard at work, questions quickly surface: *How do Counting Collections open up opportunities for these joyful and mathematically productive discussions we are hearing? What has happened in this classroom to support Deion, Astur, and their classmates to be able to work together on meaningful mathematics?* In this chapter, we will dig into these, as well as other, questions, including:

- What is the mathematics students are working on through Counting Collections?
- How do I introduce Counting Collections for the first time with my students?
- What does it look like and sound like when children get started counting together?
- How do I support students to learn how to be counting partners?
- What does recording look like with young mathematicians and why is it important?
- When and why might our class have mathematical discussions about counting?
- What logistics do I need to be thinking about as I plan for and enact Counting Collections in my classroom?
- How have primary teachers innovated with Counting Collections?

Whether Counting Collections is new to you or you have been experimenting with collections for some time, come along with us to think together about these questions.

What is the mathematics students are working on through Counting Collections?

Counting is a vibrant part of early learning about mathematics. Young children are constantly counting as they make sense of their world. How many pine cones on the ground? How many children in the circle? How many fish in the tank? Children's enthusiasm for counting can be seen in informal environments such as the playground and snack time and heard in more formal in-school experiences. We want to support young mathematicians' natural joy for counting and support important learning about number through counting.

When young mathematicians enter school, they are typically learning number names and the counting sequence. Their understanding of number can grow rapidly over the course of these early school years when they have access to, and support with, bags of collections. Through Counting Collections, and recording their counts, children have opportunities to experience quantity and develop understanding for a wide range of early ideas about number.

What early counting looks like. When young children are given a small bag of objects, it is common to observe them pour out the items and begin pointing to the scattered collection. We may see children pointing high above the items, with a bouncing finger in the air that is not yet touching the objects, and joyfully saying numbers that may or may not be in the counting sequence. As we hear such counting, "1, 2, 3, 4, 7, 10!" we can celebrate that young mathematicians are pointing and saying numbers. These children have a sense that mathematicians count things and that they point to them, saying number names. This is fertile thinking to tap into and build on!

Learning about counting and cardinality are big ideas in the early grades. Having a collection of items invites children to count to find the total number of objects. As children count, they come to understand the relationship between numbers and quantities and connect counting to cardinality. Over time, with an abundance of counting experiences, intentional partnerships, and thoughtful conversations with teachers and peers, children will say the number names in the standard order, pairing each object with one number name. They will come to understand that the last number name tells the number of objects counted and can tell *how many* items were in their collection.

Getting into the groove of counting. As children continue to develop their own strategies for touching and moving each item in their collection, important ideas about counting, cardinality, and number continue to emerge through the engaging and meaningful context of Counting Collections. For example, remember when Deion and Astur laid their collection of popsicle sticks out in a line and pointed to each stick, giving it one unique number name? This shows that these students have had experiences counting and have learned strategies for organizing and keeping track of their count. Hearing their thinking allowed their teacher to listen to the ways they are learning number names for quantities into the twenties and hear that they understand the early counting sequence. Or, remember when Deion and Astur landed on 23 and then announced there were 23 sticks? Hearing this, their teacher learned these two students show under-standing of cardinality. Deion and Astur can *see* what twenty-three things look like and use the number chart in their room to know how to write the symbol for that quantity.

More seasoned counters continue to develop number sense as they extend the counting sequence into the hundreds and learn important foundational ideas about place value. As the size of the collections grow, students encounter new opportunities and challenges. With larger quantities, students begin to think about how they can organize the items so that they can keep track and they con-sider counting by something other than ones, such as 2s, 5s, or 10s. Different tools become helpful and support mathematical understanding. The ten-frame, a hundreds chart, the number line on the wall—all of these tools support young children to reason about counting and engage in sense-making discussions about quantities and symbols for numbers in the 1s, 10s, and 100s. Children begin cre-ating their own strategies for organizing and counting, such as putting 10 in a cup. They may choose to label cups with sticky notes and then count their total by skip-counting by 10s and then 1s. It is an exciting time to reason together as a classroom community about how mathematicians call a bundle of ten 1s a *10*.

As mathematicians grow, so does the complexity of their collections. By counting up into the hundreds, children begin to find new uses for tools, such as pouring ten cups of 10 onto a plate to make groups of 100. Talk about 100s, 10s, and 1s comes alive, and the idea that a bundle of ten 10s is a *hundred* can be proved. Other groupings emerge as children get intrigued by the twenties they create from two cups of 10, or the connection they see between groups of 25s and 100s. Packaged collections, like the crayons you get at a restaurant that come four to a box, offer new mathematical situations that challenge students to consider how they want to deal with these already-existing groupings. (Since counting by 4s is tricky, how about counting 2s twice for each box? Or maybe putting a single loose crayon next to each box and making some friendly 5s?) What is unique about counting large collections is that quantities come to life, and it is powerful to *see* what big numbers look like and how they are composed. This can also sup-port students' thinking about computation and how we can use the way a number is composed or decomposed to reason when problem solving.

> **Some early number ideas that can be learned and understood through Counting Collections:**
>
> - Number names and the order of a counting sequence
> - Counting by ones and counting in groups (such as 2s, 5s, 10s, 25s, 100, and so on)
> - Seeing the relationship between quantity and the written and verbal number that expresses that quantity
> - Saying one number word for each item that is counted (one-to-one correspondence)
> - The last number you say in a counting sequence is the number of objects you have (cardinality)
> - Thinking about and figuring out *how many?* and structures that help you keep track
> - Putting together and taking apart numbers and quantities
> - Ten can be thought of as a bundle of ten 1s called a *ten*; 100 can be thought of as a bundle of ten 10s called a *hundred*
> - Understanding the operations of adding and subtracting

How do I introduce Counting Collections for the first time with my students?

Introducing Counting Collections to your young mathematicians can feel like an exciting and lively event. This activity can be introduced in many ways, and there is no particular right way. Let's drop in on Ms. Granger and her first-grade students as she introduces Counting Collections for the first time and hear how she gets things off and running.

Ms. Granger's First-Grade Classroom: Counting Collections Day 1

As Ms. Granger knelt down on the floor, her students gathered around the carpet perimeter in a circle. Ms. Granger held a collection bag and invited a colleague, Ms. Lind, the building math coach, to stop by and role-play an example of what it can look like and sound like to count a collection with a partner.

Ms. Granger: Today, mathematicians, we get to count things!

Ms. Lind: Have you ever wondered how many things you have? I've heard you wonder . . . how many fruit snacks are in a bag? How many stairs did we climb? There are lots of reasons why we count things in our everyday life. Today, we are going to begin a new activity together called Counting Collections!

Ms. Granger, (*turning to the students*)**:** When you count a collection, like this one (*holding up a collection of plastic frogs*), your job is to count how many things you have and show a picture of how many things you counted. For our first day, we are going to partner you with a classmate, hand you a collection, and invite you to go count!

As Ms. Granger and Ms. Lind introduced Counting Collections to the students, they purposefully kept the introduction brief and open ended. Instead of giving too much direction or instruction, they decided to just invite the children to *go count*! They wanted the children to think through their own decisions about how to organize their items and how to keep track. When we leave the activity open for young mathematicians to reason about structure, quantity, and organization, we allow them to problem-solve, to build on their own ideas and those of their classmates, and to grapple with what makes sense. We are also allowing students to make mathematical decisions that we can then highlight for the rest of the class. When this activity becomes too directed or structured (i.e., telling students to put their objects in a line), we take away the opportunity for students to find a need to figure these pieces out. As children count during this first day, Ms. Granger and Ms. Lind observed and listened to them to plan for future discussions, including highlighting effective partner counting strategies (e.g., children taking turns counting every other item or one child counts all the objects and the partner recounts to check).

When launching Counting Collections in your classroom, there are a few things you may want to consider beforehand. For example, having a designated table in the room where students can gather and return materials is helpful. It is also helpful to start with some available materials and to add more materials over time, as students discover a need for additional tools. (See Figures 2.2 and 2.3.)

Figure 2.2
A classroom table with materials for getting started.

Getting started materials

- Baggies of collections ranging in sizes that are a good fit for your young mathematicians
- Pencils
- Clipboards with plain paper or a recording sheet
- Hundreds chart and number line hanging on the classroom wall

Materials to offer over time

- Sticky notes (to record quantities)
- Cups (to hold 10 or more)
- Bigger containers such as plates or trays (to hold larger quantities)
- Giant ten-frames
- Laminated ten-frames
- Laminated hundred charts

Figure 2.3
A classroom table with materials that have been added to over time.

What kinds of collections should I offer my students?

In Counting Collections, it is important to respond to your students and their mathematical ideas. A good rule of thumb to start off would be to choose collections that are a bit out of reach for students. Part of the excitement of this new activity is that we are posing a big task to our young mathematicians. This might be a collection in the high teens or twenties for your new kindergarteners or a collection that crosses 100 for older students in the primary grades. You can always adjust the sizes of your collections, but if you don't start big enough, you might miss out on seeing what your young students are capable of.

Once a teacher has experience watching children count, she can then make purposeful decisions about the kinds of collections she offers to continue to extend children's mathematical understandings. For example, first grader Ari consistently lines up her objects and accurately counts one-by-one to figure out her total. This may lead her teacher to offer a bigger collection that allows Ari to think about bigger numbers and explore grouping and organizing in a different way. Kindergarten student Miles continues to feel overwhelmed with a large number of items, so his teacher may want to offer him a smaller collection that he can feel successful in completing accurately. Or she might encourage Miles to continue with his same collection but offer a tool to support his counting.

In younger grades, a teacher might consider the following questions: *Does a child show one-to-one correspondence? How far is a child counting when saying a sequence?* If a child is still working on one-to-one correspondence, a teacher may encourage the child to count again while putting the collection away one at a time into the baggie, anticipating that the motion of putting away will help the child count just one number for each item. Or the teacher might consider how the type of item supports the student to count, such as counting bears that children like to stand up one by one while counting. If a child is counting well but still skipping some of those tricky teen numbers, we might offer a collection into the high twenties or thirties, since the numbers above 20 become regular again. A teacher should think about an ambitious quantity (go for it!), but pay attention that it isn't too overwhelming. There is also space for students to select their own collections and then learn within their experiences what might be a best fit for them at any given time.

Teachers can always take the lead from their students. If they want to choose a bag that feels higher, let them try. The way their eyes light up when they have counted "the most things ever!" is totally worth it. A teacher may also tailor the size of the collection to the big mathematical ideas he and the children are working on in class. For example, if the class is working on a unit with larger numbers, they might have class discussions about larger quantity collections, or if they are working on a unit that focuses on computation and word problems within 100, engaging in collections of less than 100 can help in thinking about the ideas of "How many more to 100?" Realistically, Counting Collections could be a mainstay that can be adjusted to support any part of a curriculum. For example, kindergarteners could count smaller collections than usual to think about representing different problem situations. First graders could count collections that are useful when they first start to really concentrate on place value and building numbers to 100; this could be more or less than what they have been using to simply count. Second graders may be focused on thinking about subtraction, so their teacher may have them count collections and then pose a follow-up question to the count, such as *If you lost _____ from your collection, how many would you have then?* Collections could be a springboard for other problem situations (equal sharing, comparing subsets within the collection), thinking about arrays, focusing on the structure of two-digit or three-digit numbers when they are new and students need to see quantities and experience how they are acted on in problem-solving situations.

Beginning collections in your classroom is lively and can call on you to have a spirit of adventure. The key is to get structures in place (e.g., routines for where to get materials and how to work with a partner) while allowing the activity to be open ended and student centered. Our goal is to open up opportunities for young mathematicians to experience joy and wonder for quantity, counting, and coming to know the number sequence and symbols.

What does it look like and sound like when children get started counting together?

As Counting Collections becomes a regular activity in your classroom, many routines can be put in place to support a quality chunk of time during which children can really dig into their collections—counting and recording—and the teacher can interact with children around their counting. You might precede Counting Collections with a brief discussion that raises new questions or highlights particular strategies children were trying during the last counting time. The day might end with the group coming back together to wrap up, share, and highlight big ideas from the day.

In the beginning, supporting children to know how to get started is an important consideration. Let's go back into Ms. Granger's classroom a few days later to see how students begin a Counting Collections session.

Ms. Granger's First-Grade Classroom: Counting Collections Day 3

After a whole-class discussion about how students have been counting and organizing their objects, Ms. Granger sends the children off. She reminds the children they will gather again in a bit to share their recordings and the tools they are using.

Ms. Granger kneels down next to Jaylen to remind him what a partner does. "Remember, Jaylen, you are Partner A so your job is to get the collection and the counting tools. Jasper will get the recording materials and find a spot since he is Partner B. Next you need to decide how you might group your count. Let's get started."

In one part of the room, Kai quickly grabs a collection out of the blue bin that Ms. Granger directed him toward and heads over to his partner, Steven, who has chosen their favorite counting spot by the reading corner. As they get settled in to count, they discuss how they want to group their collection today.

"Let's put 10 in a cup," suggests Kai.

"No, I think we should put 5 in a cup," says Steven.

"Oh yeah, okay, we haven't done 5s in a while," Kai excitedly says. The boys get to work counting their collection into cups of 5. (See Figure 2.4.)

Figure 2.4
Kai and Steven use their cups to keep track of groups of 5.

Nearby, Dina is walking back and forth between her desk and a different spot on the carpet. She is having difficulty determining where she wants to count her collection with her partner, Naomi. Finally, Naomi convinces her to sit on the rug, and they start discussing how they want to count today.

"Let's put each one on a square of our hundreds chart, like this," suggests Dina.

Figure 2.5
Naomi and Dina use ten-frames to count their collections.

"That is too hard," says Naomi. "They don't fit on their spot. Let's do ten-frames and count by 2s." Their discussion continues as they get their recording sheets ready. (See Figure 2.5.)

As groups settle in, a few students pop up again to grab forgotten supplies, such as a clipboard, a pencil, a ten-frame. Throughout the hustle and bustle of gathering supplies, Ms. Granger has been quietly reminding students how to get started—finding a spot that works for them and what it looks like to work together. Pretty soon the room is filled with the sound of objects being organized as well as students counting out loud and talking through their counting decisions. As in many classrooms, Ms. Granger's students know that they can count as many collections as they want to during this time. Since it is early on in their year, they know that Ms. Granger likes to check-in with them before they move on to a new collection, and they look forward to sharing with her the counting they have completed.

* * *

Counting Collections is a lively time. Students are doing a variety of things all around the classroom. Ultimately, students have freedom within a structure; they have been given some ideas about how to get going right away and how to settle disagreements. Teachers just starting Counting Collections might want to consider the following:

- Where can students count (or it might be easier to simply discuss where *not* to count)?
- What kind of an organization system do you want for your materials (tools, collections, recording sheets, pencils, clipboards)?

- What is a productive noise level during Counting Collections? Counting Collections is active and loud, but a conversation about the limits of the noise might be beneficial. Be prepared to accept more noise in return for highly engaged and mathematically productive students.
- What do students do when they are done counting and recording? Count their collection again in a different way? Clean up and get a new collection? Wait for a teacher check-in? Find another student who is also finished so they can share about their recordings?
- What will cleanup look and sound like at the end of collections time? This can often become a challenge as students work to put a lot of materials away. How might you structure it?

How do I support students to learn how to be counting partners?

We recommend children count collections in partners. Learning mathematics is a social activity, and counting together creates meaningful opportunities for students to learn with and from each other. Children benefit from hearing the ideas of others and working with a peer who can support their thinking and learning. Thinking through a plan together can allow students to see that there are many different ways to problem-solve. You may also discover that students occasionally benefit from individual counting opportunities. We've learned that every so often teachers find it helpful to invite students to count on their own in order to get a sense of what a student can do independently.

Another consideration is how to pair up your students. It can be done in many ways, but it seems the more intentional the partnership, the more mathematically productive students end up being. If, for example, you have a kindergarten student who gets stuck in the counting sequence at transitions to landmark numbers, such as 29 to 30, he or she could be partnered with a student who knows the counting sequence; this becomes a natural support for the first student. Or you might have a student who has just begun to think about quantity in units (2s, 5s, 10s) and can articulate why this might be a more efficient way to count; if you partner this student with another student who hasn't had this idea yet, they can now support each other in thinking about more complex mathematical ideas.

As we get to know our students as mathematicians, we begin to notice that some students have strong ideas about how quantities and numbers work and can verbally explain their reasoning; we might want to pair this student with another who is a curious and strong counter. This would help them to think about and see, "What are we doing here, and why is this counting we are doing important and even fun?" We also might notice students who haven't had as many opportunities to work collaboratively on a mathematical activity. These students may need additional support with what it means to be a partner or how to collaboratively count together rather than one partner shouldering all the work. These students would be more successful if partnered with another student who exhibits patience and willingness to hold his or her partner accountable to being a learner.

Partnering can be quite a multifaceted decision for teachers as they consider students' mathematical habits of mind, social needs, and counting skills. Whether you have been Counting Collections for a while with your students or this is your first go at it, you will quickly recognize that there are some really successful partnerships and some that, for various reasons, just don't quite work out. We, as teachers, can support successful partnerships through whole-group lessons: *How can we make sure both partners are counting?* or *How can we make decisions together about how or what we count?* And, when students are counting, we can have direct conversations in the moment with them: *How will you count this collection? Is there a way you can count together? How did you two decide what to count by?* Other questions that encourage students to examine their work as partners include: *How can you be a good math partner? What might it look like to count together?*

What does recording look like with young mathematicians, and why is it important?

Often teachers of young children wonder about the role of recording and find themselves on the fence about when to invite children to record and why. You may also wonder about how to support students to record while also leaving the choices about recording up to them.

In our experience, supporting primary students to record their ideas is an important part of Counting Collections. The recordings serve as a window into children's thinking and become an artifact that allows a classroom of young mathematicians to discuss their own and one another's ideas. From their drawings, we can ask students questions about their thinking, and they can share their work as a way to talk about their ideas. Recording can start right away; oftentimes, a blank piece of paper and a pencil are best. Keeping it simple, you can invite students to record by asking them to show how many they counted. As you check in with them about how they're counting their collections, make sure to check in about their recordings as well. Sometimes a conversation with the whole class before or after, discussing students' recording sheets and their strategies for recording, allows students to share with one another basic ways of showing their count, such as tally marks or drawing a 10 in a circle to represent 10 in a cup. Allowing the ideas to emerge from students' own recording sheets helps us to share student-generated recording strategies instead of planting the seeds for those recording strategies ourselves.

Recordings also serve as an opportunity for young mathematicians to learn how to write number symbols. For example, remember in the opening vignette when Deion and Astur went to the hundreds chart to see how to write *23*? As they recorded their total, they got practice in writing numbers and representing a number of objects with a written numeral.

In early grades, recordings often begin with a few marks on a page (see also Chapter 6, "Preschool Connections"). The marks may be different lengths going in different directions and spread out on the page. We want to embrace and celebrate early renditions of children's recordings! Within these drawings are important insights into children's mathematical thinking. Recording ideas as a mathematician is something we can work on together over time, and there is no pressure for what it should look like.

Next, we share several examples of what children's recordings may look like over the course of kindergarten through second grade. As you study the students' work, see whether you can make sense of the recording: How did the pair of children record? What symbols did they use? What was their total? How does their recording communicate how they counted? And for the older children, how did they organize their ideas? (See Figures 2.6 to 2.10.) We also offer a few different blank recording sheets for teachers to select from, try, and adapt in Appendix 1.

When and why might our class have mathematical discussions about counting?

Counting Collections is ripe for mathematical discussions. When and why you have those discussions can be quite varied. It's really about harnessing the power of the activity to raise important noticings and learnings about mathematical content and practices.

You may choose to have discussions before, during, and after a counting session. A discussion beforehand allows you to raise ideas before children dig into counting for the day. For example, you may have observed an effective way children have been organizing their counts and you want to invite students to model that strategy. Or maybe you have noticed children beginning to use a new tool, such as the ten-frame, and you think the class would benefit from talking about how to use that tool as they count. A discussion beforehand is a great way to introduce new ideas for children to consider that day.

At other times, you may want to pause counting amid the activity and invite the class to consider something you are noticing. For example, some students may have decided to organize their count in a way others haven't seen before. Or maybe some students are using a tool in a new way. These midcount conversations can support students in seeing their peers in action and provide them with an opportunity to try out a new idea immediately.

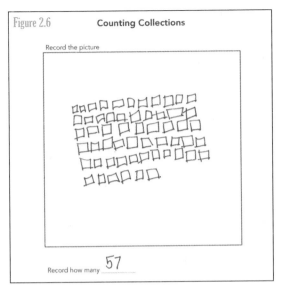

Figure 2.6 **Counting Collections**

Record the picture

Record how many 57

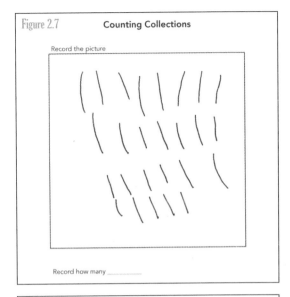

Figure 2.7 **Counting Collections**

Record the picture

Record how many _____

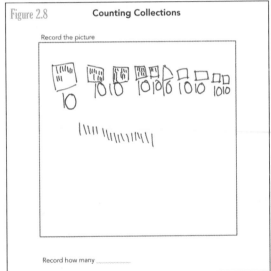

Figure 2.8 **Counting Collections**

Record the picture

Record how many _____

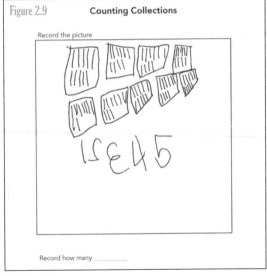

Figure 2.9 **Counting Collections**

Record the picture

Record how many _____

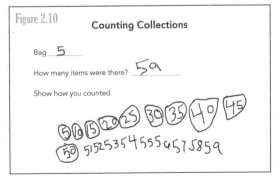

Figure 2.10 **Counting Collections**

Bag __5__

How many items were there? 59

Show how you counted

Examples of student recordings.

Another opportune time for discussion is at the end of a counting session. This is an ideal time for anchoring some learning that can be built on for next time, posing a reflective question that might help students think about a new idea, or highlighting some student ideas or thinking that others would benefit from hearing. Examples could include exhibiting students' different methods of recording—one student may represent his or her count with tally marks, another student uses the numeral 10—and then prompting students to make connections across why students might want to show these quantities in different ways. Another example could be to save a group's collection exactly as they counted it and have students count in whole group to talk about the counting transition we make when we count by hundreds and then tens and then ones.

Many discussions will be whole group; however, you can also find richness in small-group discussions. Maybe you are kneeling down with one pair of children and you invite another pair close to you to join the conversation. Or perhaps a pair of students are struggling and you invite them to go on a walk around the classroom with you to observe other children at work. These tailored conversations allow for more intentional teaching, assessing, and questioning to take place. Often, we teachers are looking for ways to support students in a more individualized way. While other students are around the room, engaged in counting with their partners, it is often a perfect time for teachers to drop in to collect information about their students. These conversations range from listening to students count and asking questions about their thinking, to supporting students in remembering what their resources are for counting or recording. Some examples of further conversations follow.

Social Goals	Sounds Like
Support students to count together.	"How will you count this collection?" "Is there a way you can count together?" "How did you both decide together what to count by?" "How can you make decisions together?"
Encourage pairs of students to make connections between their two representations.	"Are your representations the same?" "How are your recordings different?"
Productive work.	"How can you be a good math partner?" "How can you make sure you both are learning and counting?" "What might it look like to count together?"

Recording Goals	Sounds Like
Prompt students to decide how they can record how many items there were on paper.	"Okay, so you counted how many. Now can you show on paper how many there are? Try to write it so someone can see exactly how you counted."
Students may need support in writing numbers.	"Wow, 120. Do you know how to write that number? Let's see if we can find a resource that will help us see what that number looks like." "Can you read these to me?" "What does that number look like when you write it?"
Ask students to explain the meaning of their representation.	"Tell me about what you've written here. How many does it show?" "Does your picture match what your count looks like?"
Press students to explain connections between their representation and the physical items.	"Are you sure that is how many there are? How do you know?" "Is there a way you could make it clearer?" "It looks like you drew a circle for each one, does that match how you counted?"

Counting Goals	Sounds Like
Prompt students to decide what to count by and how to organize the count.	"It looks like you are just getting started. Do you know what you are going to count by today?" "Is there a tool you might use to help you keep track or stay organized?" "Hmm . . . counting by 1s is taking you a while, isn't it? Is there a faster way you could count how many there are?"
Supporting misconceptions or miscounts, i.e., transitions from decades (29, 30, or 39, 40).	"Is there a tool that could help you to know what the next number is?" Partner with a student who knows the counting sequence

(continued)

Support students to complete their count. Students may get stuck at a particular number or lose track of which items have been counted.	"Do you think there's a way we could keep track to be sure to count each one?" "How are you going to keep track of each of your 5s?"
Check for cardinality after they count.	"So, how many are there?" Students may either state the final number (showing understanding of cardinality) or be somewhat puzzled or just start counting the set again.
Check for accuracy, counting sequence, and understanding of quantity.	"How many do you have?" "What did your counting sound like? Can I listen to you count?" "How many are in this cup? Why did you put 10?" "It sounds like/looks like you revised your thinking. Can you tell me more about that?"

The open nature of counting allows us to listen to the sense our students are making and talk with them about their ideas, whether one-on-one, in small groups, or with the entire class.

The nature of the discussions can shift over time. In the beginning of Counting Collections with your students, the discussions can tend to be about navigating the social aspects of counting together with a partner. For example, early on you might find yourself discussing how to work with partners in mathematically productive ways and create an anchor chart that children can refer to. After that, you may talk about how to make decisions as partner teams and invite students to role-play making decisions together. From there, you may find it helpful to discuss what students can do if they have a disagreement and engage children in brainstorming ways to solve problems that may arise. Eventually, you can nurture discussions about how children have conversations about their mathematical ideas and think together about what questions they might ask one another to hear one another's thinking. Sentence stems such as *How do you want to count today? I don't understand . . .* or *Can I show you my idea . . .* can be especially helpful in supporting young mathematicians to share and hear one another's ideas.

Here, we drop in on Mr. Crandall's second-grade class, busily counting their collections that range between 100 and 300 things. We move in to listen to Jayden and Nyjaun and the mathematical work that they can accomplish together, cultivated by a classroom environment that has supported them to have productive conversations about their mathematical ideas. They are double-checking their collection of twelve cups of ten marbles each and two more marbles:

Jayden, (*pointing to cups of 10 marbles as he counts*): . . . 50, 60, 70, 80, 90, 100, 110, 120 (*points to marbles in his hand*) 121, 122.

Nyjaun: No, it's 130, 140 (*pointing to the 2 marbles in Jayden's hands*)!

Jayden: Nooooo, 'cause look, 10, 20, 30 (*recounts marbles, same as before, and Nyjaun joins in until they are counting single objects*) 121 (*holds up 1 marble*), 122 (*holds up other marble*).

Nyjaun: No, it's 130, 140.

Jayden: No because there's only 2 left. And you have to have 10 marbles (*holds up a cup of 10*). We would need 2 more 10s, but we have 1s.

Nyjaun: It's 140.

Jayden: It would have to be 10 more to be 130 and then 10 more to be 140. Or we would need 8 more to have 10 here (*holding up 2 singles*). But we only have 2.

Nyjaun: Wait, let me count again. 10, 20, 30, 40, 50, 60, 70, 80, 90, 100, 110, 120 . . . wait 10, 20 (*counts all over by 10s*), but it goes 130, 140.

Jayden: But we would need 10, we only have 1 (*holding up 1 marble*). So it's 121, 122. It would be 130, then 140 if we had 10s. You're right that is the way we would count if we had more 10s. But we don't, we just have 1s. That's why we have to switch to saying 121, 122.

Nyjaun: Ohhhhhhhh, I was counting like we did altogether as a class the other day, but I guess we were just counting by 10s then. There were not any more 1s, only 10s. Today there are 1s *and* 10s. (See Figure 2.11.)

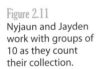
Figure 2.11
Nyjaun and Jayden work with groups of 10 as they count their collection.

As counting becomes more routine in your classroom, and the social aspects are under way, the discussion of mathematics takes stronger hold. Early discussions may focus on strategies students are using for organizing and counting their objects. For example, what does it look like and sound like to count one object and point to each object as you go. Or, how are students keeping track of the ones they already counted? Using the students' recording sheets or photos of their collections as artifacts, you can open up discussions to share drawings of the counts. How are children showing how many? Why do mathematicians use symbols (such as tally marks) to represent an item instead of drawing the item in detail? Or let's look at Fabian and Zara's recording and see whether we can tell how many items were in their collection. You may also find yourself discussing accuracy. What does the word *accurate* mean? Why is it important to be accurate when we count? How can we make sure our total is accurate? What tools help us count accurately? While accuracy is important in counting, we caution against making accuracy the ultimate focus. Remember part of the beauty of Counting Collections is opening up opportunities for young mathematicians to experience the joy and wonder for counting. Too narrow of a focus on accuracy can zap that joy and wonder.

To see a mathematical discussion brought to life, let's join Ms. Spencer and her first-grade students, as they have a whole-class discussion at the end of a counting session. During the session, Ms. Spencer noticed that some students were beginning to use cups as a tool to organize their counting. As she listened to students Izzie and Fiona using this tool, she paid attention to why they were using the cups. She overheard them saying, "Let's pour our filled ten-frame into a cup. Then we can use the ten-frame over again, and then we can count the cups by 10s. And we can keep track of where we are!" She had observed several pairs of students start their count over because they forgot what number they were on. As the size of the collections were getting bigger, it was becoming more and more common for students to get lost as they filled ten-frames. As Izzie and Fiona begin counting 10 into a cup, and filling cups of 10, Ms. Spencer was excited this strategy was emerging. She thought it was a good next step for her student as they worked to make sense of 10 as a unit. She was hoping this would come about, but she didn't want the idea to be teacher directed.

Why put ten in a cup?

Ms. Spencer: Izzie and Fiona, as I was watching you count your collection of glass beads today, I noticed that you were using a new tool to help you. I noticed that you were using a cup. Can you tell us more about why you used a cup and how it helped you?

Figure 2.12
Fiona and Izzie puzzle through how to use the ten-frame.

Izzie: We started using a cup today because we needed somewhere to put our things after the ten-frame was filled. (See Figure 2.12.)

Ms. Spencer: So, the cup was a place to put your glass beads after you had filled a ten-frame. I see. Fiona, do you want to add on to that?

Fiona: Um, we were putting them in piles. We were sliding the beads off of the ten-frame into piles, and then we knew those piles were 10. But when we moved around some of the beads, then we didn't know how many we had.

Ms. Spencer: Okay, so we hear you saying that the cups were a place to be sure you had 10 (*turning to the class*). What questions do you have for Izzie and Fiona about how or why they used the cups?

Vivienne: Where did you find the cups?

Izzie: They are over there on the table.

Ms. Spencer: I'm so glad you asked that Vivienne. Class, we have cups available to help you organize your count if you would like to begin experimenting with them.

What logistics do I need to be thinking about as I plan for and enact Counting Collections in my classroom?

Now that we have thought about the rich mathematical opportunities within Counting Collections, let's turn to thinking together about the logistics. While Counting Collections is an open-ended, student-centered activity, there are several management and planning issues that are helpful to think through ahead of time. As you get started, it is important to think about ideas such as:

- Where in the classroom will children count?
- How will children get their materials?
- How will I partner students? Why?
- When children finish a count, how do they transition to a next count?
- What does a wrap-up look like?

As collections get under way, you can use what you are learning from listening to your students to think about upcoming sessions. You may ask yourself, *How did my plan play out during our last counting session? What parts might I need to tweak today and why? As children are counting today, what am I going to be paying attention to and listening for? What questions will I ask? Are the sizes of the collections well matched to my students and their understanding of counting?* Since listening to your student count reveals important insights into their current understandings, you can also plan for how you can take note of what you are learning about students' thinking. How might I record what I'm noticing about students' thinking? Are students engaged in mathematically productive activity? Are students spending their time counting and talking about their counting? Are students making sense of the collection they have and the recording they are doing?

How have primary teachers innovated with Counting Collections?

Counting Collections is ripe for innovating. Just as the activity is open ended for children to devise new ways for counting, it is open for teachers to be creative as well. We have seen brilliant ways that teachers have taken this activity and adapted it, in response to what they are learning about their students. In this section, we will highlight some innovations we have learned about from teachers, such as *How Many More to 100? Adding Collections,* and *Counting Packaged Collections.* Hopefully, the descriptions and vignettes will inspire you to try these ideas and come up with your own adaptations to design new mathematical opportunities for children.

How Many More to 100?

In Ms. Tse's first grade, students had been Counting Collections every Wednesday all school year. On this day, midway into the year, students were Counting Collections that were less than 100, sorting their collections in ways that made sense to them, and figuring out how many items were in their collection. After they determined how many objects were in their collection, they had an additional step—to figure out how many more objects they need to get to 100.

Ms. Tse, *kneeling down next to Ismail and Alicia*: How many did you have in your collections?

Ismail: 75.

Ms. Tse: You had 75? All right, so now we want to figure out how many more you would need to get to 100. How can you figure that out?

Alicia: We can get a hundreds chart, and then we can count all the way to 100.

Ms. Tse: Okay, do that and I will come back to hear your thinking.

As Ms. Tse knelt down next to different pairs of children, she saw students using hundreds charts in various ways. One pair of children pointed to their total on the chart, and then they counted on to 100, pointing to each successive number until they got to 100. Another pair of students laid their items on the hundreds chart and then pointed to each number on the chart until they got to 100. A third pair of students did not use a hundreds chart; rather, on their recording sheet, they started with their total and added on by drawing circles until they got to 100, and then they went back to count how many circles they had drawn. Ms. Tse chose to invite students to share this range of strategies in a whole-group discussion to culminate the collections time (view the video of these interactions at https://www.teachingchannel.org/videos/counting-by-ten-lesson). She emphasized to the students that they had done a great job making sense of this problem and persevering in solving the problem.

Adding Collections

Mrs. Williams's first-grade class has just begun a unit that focuses on thinking about place value while adding two-digit numbers. Once a week during this unit, Mrs. Williams has planned to have each student in a pair count part of their collection on her own and then add together the parts of the collections. She explains to the students that today they will work together a little differently; she walks them through the logistics of getting a bag (all bags are under 75 objects) with their partner, getting a recording sheet, and each partner counting his or her own part of the collection and organizing it by 10s and 1s. After both partners has found the total of their part, they work together to figure out how many total objects they started with in their bag. As the students begin,

Mrs. Williams stands back as everyone gets settled in. She begins to walk around the room, listening to partners and noticing where she can begin to ask questions to dig into her students' thinking.

Mrs. Williams: Sawyer and Landon, tell me about your counting so far.

Landon: Well, she is counting hers in a cup and I am counting mine, but I don't get how we are going to find out how many we have altogether if we don't count them altogether.

Mrs. Williams: Hmm, well when you are finished counting all your objects, let me know and I would love to hear how you problem-solve that together.

Mrs. Williams moves on to another group and then sees Sawyer raise her hand to let her know they are finished counting.

Sawyer: We are all done. So, what do we do now?

Mrs. Williams: My question to the class was, how many objects do you have altogether? So, if someone asked you, how many do you and Landon have together, what would you say?

Sawyer: Well, he has 34, and I have 21.

Landon: She said together, but we don't have them together. We counted apart like you said to.

Mrs. Williams: Hmm, so I'm wondering, is there a way you could find out how many together?

Sawyer: Can we move them? Like, can I put mine over by his?

Mrs. Williams: It seems like that might be a good idea.

Sawyer: 'Cause if we put them together, we can put the 10 cups together and the 1s together.

Mrs. Williams: Why don't you do that, and I will come check on you in a bit to see what you have found out.

Mrs. Williams moves on to another group that she can hear counting together.

Mrs. Williams: Logan and Amelia, can you count that out loud one more time so I can listen to you?

The two students have already determined that they can put their two collections together and then count by 10s and 1s. She is noticing that they are unsure of how to record what they have done.

Logan: We got 63 things, but how do we show what we did? Do we just draw
    10s and 1s?

Mrs. Williams: You could.

Amelia: But how do we show that he had these (*pointing to some cups*), and I
    had these (*pointing to the rest*)? Can we draw them separate?

Mrs. Williams: You could, as long as you also show how many there are
    altogether.

This Counting Collections innovation provides so many wonderful opportunities for discussions about place value and how we can represent addition, and
even leads to some conversations about parts and wholes.

Counting Packaged Collections

We have been inspired by the ways teachers offer packaged collections to young
mathematicians. Packages of collections could be plastic-wrapped crayons in 2s
and 4s, raffle tickets in strips of 5s, paper cutouts of hands (count the fingers).
For example, in Ms. Allen's classroom, she offers packaged collections to push
students to think about other kinds of groups beyond 1s and 10s. One day, after
sharing with her students that she found some crayons that came in packs of 2,
she hands a container of the packaged crayons to Ava and asks her to take a try
at counting the collection.

Ms. Allen, *passing the container to Ava*: Ava, what do you notice about these
    crayons?

Ava: I notice they are blue and green. I notice they are in packs of 2s. Okay, I
    can count by 2s!

Ms. Allen: Ah, okay.

Ava: 2, 4, 6, 8, 10, 12, 14 (*pausing with her hand on her head*), 16, 18, 20, 22, 24,
    25, 26 (*pointing to each individual crayon in the pack*), 27, 28, 29, 30, 31, 32.

Ms. Allen: How many crayons are there?

Ava: 32!

Ms. Allen: How did you count them?

Ava: By 2, but then I counted by 1s.

Ms. Allen: Why did you switch from counting by 2s to counting by 1s?

Ava: I didn't know what came next in 2s, but I could see the crayons in the
    see-through package, so I pointed to each crayon and kept going.

Ms. Allen: I see. I hear you saying you're counting by 2s and by 1s. I'm
    wondering, could you organize your count in any other ways?

Ava, (*pausing and looking at the packages; she begins pushing packages together*): 2, 4, 6, 8, 10. That's 10 together; 2, 4, 6, 8, 10. That's another 10; 2, 4, 6, 8, 10. Another 10. That's (*pointing to the piles of 10*) 10, 20, 30, and then this package is 31, 32.

Ms. Allen: Wow, that is some great thinking.

In this episode, Ms. Allen uses packaged crayons in clear wrappers so that each individual item is visible. Having these objects in groups pushed Ava to count by 2s. Being able to see each item supported her to continue counting on by 1s in a way that she might not have been able to if the crayons were in opaque cardboard boxes.

Conclusion

Counting Collections opens up a wide range of learning opportunities for children of all ages, particularly for children in the primary grades. The openness of the activity allows young mathematicians to make mathematical and social decisions, such as how to count, organize objects, use tools, keep track of totals, show their thinking, engage with others' ideas, and work collaboratively with other mathematicians. And the routine nature of the activity provides a structure that supports student learning, teacher learning, and innovation. We hope that the ideas in this chapter inspire you and your students to delve into Counting Collections and experience wonder and joy together. (See Appendix 3 for links to videos and blog posts that show Counting Collections in action with young children.)

CHAPTER 3

Counting Collections 3–5

by Julie Kern Schwerdtfeger and
Darlene Fish Doto

Marcos bends eye level to the table, sees that his towers of 20 are not quite even in height, evens out the tiles, recounts his total, and keeps building. At the next table, Layla and Esmeralda slide sunflower seeds quickly by 2s, dropping 10 at a time into cups of tens. They then stack 10 cups together to make a different kind of tower. Nearby, Richard and Elian are at the supply cabinet, creating an inventory sheet for the teacher, listing the markers and other supplies the class will use this year. The teacher has requested an exact count of everything. In the courtyard, Theo is stacking milk crates. His teacher steps outside to ask, "Did you find Mr. Castro and figure out how many milk cartons are delivered in a crate?" They begin a conversation about what Theo learned in the front office and how the quantity of milk consumed each week at the school seems to vary.

Why is the teacher investing valuable time having her third and fourth graders count, when they seem to have already accomplished rich counting tasks with such enthusiasm and skill in earlier grades? What more are they learning if we extend their counting tasks into the upper elementary grades?

The large majority of our upper grade students have learned one-to-one correspondence as they count discrete items, can usually group items efficiently, can call numbers in order even when they skip count, and can enthusiastically count to high numbers. Each of these accomplishments is the result of their rich experiences counting and building number sense in primary classrooms. In the upper grades, we also see daily evidence that they put their counting skills to use when they problem-solve, for example, when we hear them add three 10s to 148, raising a finger for each ten as they go: "158, 168, 178." We are tempted to believe "counting" is a fait accompli. They can count; they certainly were taught well!

Before we race forward though, let's be sure that our students are indeed standing on solid ground. We may at times be tempted to feel that we don't have *time* to revisit things that teachers in the earlier grades were meant to have covered, but the truth is, children may not be finished with these tasks. Furthermore, Counting Collections in the upper grades provides a meaningful context in which students can grapple with foundational mathematical principles and properties. The benefits come from both the continuity (revisiting counting tasks they are familiar with) and the stretch toward more demanding counting and recording. In other words, there is merit in spiraling back to Counting Collections.

To do so with confidence, we as teachers have to believe in the complexity of the math the children undertake and see how it matches well with our goals. So, our first priority in this chapter is to investigate the mathematics that children dive into when they count.

As upper-grade teachers, we may find what children do both underwhelming and overwhelming. Sometimes, we see students revisit tasks they already tackled in earlier grades, but we may find that they struggle more than we expected. At other times, the math they're doing matches the curriculum of third, fourth, and fifth grade well. We are satisfied when we see multiplication sentences emerge in recordings, for example. And sometimes we see students connect their collection counting with complex mathematics that surpasses what we expected them to be able to take on in elementary school. Counting Collections is a task that truly offers multiple entry points.

Let's take a look into third-, fourth-, and fifth-grade classrooms where students are invited to count large collections together. We will enter busy classrooms where students are intently focused. We will see them set their own tasks with peers, negotiate plans, organize large collections of objects, count out loud, draw and write to record, talk through differences, overcome setbacks, and persevere. We will hear them count to high numbers and write many numbers down as they go in order to keep track and, ultimately, use them to record complex number sentences.

We will hear a lot of conversation and notice that the mathematicians are having fun. We will celebrate that everyone has a place to start and feels successful with the tasks; we want children to feel competent as a fresh new school year unfolds. We see friendships and academic partnerships being formed between new classmates, and we know as teachers that these relationships will strengthen our communities throughout the year. Let's begin by investigating the mathematics behind Counting Collections in the upper grades.

Marisol and Eva: Strengthening Relationships Between Tens and Hundreds

In the following scenario, two eight-year-old girls are working together to further develop a deeper understanding of a large number: 349. A student entering third grade is still working on an understanding of place value. The following opportunity gives them a chance to construct and see how many groups of 10 are in that big number (34) and then to rearrange their collection to show how many hundreds (3) are in that number as well. The "doing" helps them build a relationship with this quantity that simply working on paper cannot. The girls also have an opportunity to help each other skip-count by 10s across the hundreds, something we discover is not as easy as expected.

Marisol and Eva approach the table covered in baskets and tins of items to count. They both eye the colorful buttons and decide to work together for the morning. Clearing a space on a table, they negotiate a starting point. They agree to group the buttons by tens and begin covering the table with 5-by-2 arrangements. (See Figures 3.1 and 3.2.) They work side by side from opposite ends of

Figure 3.1
Organizing buttons with 5-by-2 arrangements.

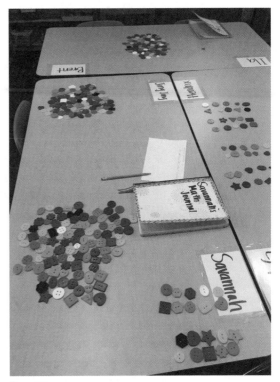

Figure 3.2
Combined arrangements into 10 tens or 100.

the table, each counting out loud, but without derailing each other. They count over and over by twos: "2, 4, 6, 8, 10." All of the buttons are finally organized and out of the basket. In spite of the time it takes to lay out all of the groups, the work so far has been easily managed.

The girls now need a total, and they begin counting in unison by tens, pointing to the groups as they go. But there are counting errors on Eva's part: "70, 80, 90, 100, 200, 300 . . ."

Marisol hesitates. "No, it's 80, 90, 100, 110 . . ."

Past 100, Eva is less sure of herself. But with Marisol's support, she continues. The girls finish their count together and write down 349.

Their teacher, Ms. Morchower, comes over and asks the girls to show her how many there are and wonders aloud whether there is another way they can show their total. When she leaves, the girls push 10 groups of 10 together to make piles of 100s and place pencils between their 100s, 10s, and "extras."

One may be tempted to think that the girls are putting to work what they already know about groups of 10s and 100s. But Eva's counting needed practice. And the task of organizing their collection quickly, efficiently, accurately, and collaboratively inside of a math hour, and in two different ways, would not have come easily when they were younger. The girls are continuing to build a relationship with quantities such as 349, and in this classroom, they will be problem-solving and working with big numbers all year.

Manuel, Noah, and Max: Developing a Sense of Quantity and Number Relations

In the following scenario, three boys in fourth grade are constructing number relations through the estimates they make about their collection. We also witness them engage in rich mathematical reasoning. The investigation is sparked by a teacher's question, posed when they were in the middle of counting their collection.

In the library corner, Manuel, Noah, and Max are counting flat marbles. Manuel is making groups of tens on the table. Max is walking five groups at a time from the table to the rug. Noah is acting as a double-checker and changes the groups that have 49 or 52 in them into an accurate 50 as they are delivered by Max. After some back and forth, they agree that they now have 250 marbles on the floor, with plenty remaining on the table. (See Figure 3.3.) Ms. Morchower stops by to ask them to estimate their total. "If this is 250, considering how many are left on the table, how many do you think you will have in all?" Manuel responds, "I think we will have 625." Max chimes in, "I think maybe

Figure 3.3
How can we be sure
there are 250
marbles here?

750 to 800, because it looks like we counted about a third of everything." Noah says, "I think 3,000! It looks like a lot."

What do the boys reveal that they know in making their estimates? That the group still to be counted is larger than the group already counted. Manuel posits that inside of 625 there are two full groups of 250, plus about half that many again. Max thinks they have only counted a third of the whole and knows that 3 times 250 is 750. Noah does not give such careful consideration to what is on the table but thinks of a "big number." Completing the count not only provides support for their own developing theories about quantity but also affords the boys the chance to hear and consider one another's thinking. It gives them a chance to articulate number relations. For example, seeing how large his pile of 250 looked in relation to the remaining marbles allows Manuel to make a conjecture about the relationship between 250 and 625. This type of reasoning will serve him well when he operates on numbers.

The development of number sense does not happen in isolation in this classroom. On display in the library corner is Bruce Goldstone's book, *Great Estimations*. Ms. Morchower has been sharing a few pages each day during the daily math warm-up time. She also regularly projects photographs of collections counted during math, for students to compare and discuss. For example, one day she projects a picture of 250 seeds and of 250 flat marbles that were counted at different tables. She asks the class open-ended questions to elicit their observations and thoughts, "What do you notice?" and "How can we be sure that both of these collections represent 250?" This teacher is in the habit of working conversations about numbers into her classroom regularly. Whether the numbers arise in the classroom, in the larger school environment, or are found in current events, in literature, or in science, her students do a lot of talking about numbers. Even this early in the year, these short, thoughtful conversations captivate student attention and may well have helped the boys reason through their estimations in the ways that they did.

Maya and Alex: Building and Writing Big Numbers

In this conversation with their teacher, two students grapple with how to write numbers bigger than they have written before. Instead of being shown or told how to do it, the teacher holds back and lets them think it through and use what they know how to figure out what they do not yet know.

Maya and Alex are moving all of the yellow "flats," representing 100 each, out of a large basket and stacking them into cubes of 1,000. Maya diligently recounts the total each time Alex adds another 1,000 to the table, tapping her pencil on top of the stacks to keep track. She ultimately records 1,000 four times, then doubles her 4,000 to get to 8,000, matching exactly how she counted her collection. From there, she counts up by 1,000. She now has to figure out a way to record 9,000, 10,000, 11,000, 12,000. There are three extra flats as well.

Alex: We have 1,000, 2,000, 3,000, 4,000, 5,000, 6,000, 7,000, 8,000, 9,000, 10,000, 11,000, 12,000, and 3.

Maya: No, that's not 3. And don't tell me! Now I have to add these 4,000 to these 4,000. That means 4,000 plus another 4,000. That's 8,000.

Alex: Maya, you could just count this (*indicates the piles*) and then it's a lot faster: 1, 2, 3, 4, 5, 6, 7, 8, 9, 10, 11, 12.

Maya: Yeah, but I need to show the work. We need to write it down. So, 8,000 plus four more thousand. Nine thousand (*writes* 9,000), ten thousand (*hesitates*). How do you write ten thousand?
(*The teacher has walked over to the children and is observing.*)

Teacher: That's a really good question. Alex maybe you can help us. How do you write ten thousand?
(*Alex writes* 1,000 *in his math journal.*)

Teacher: Hmm, that's going to be *one thousand*.

Maya: Oh! I know! (*writes* 1,010)

Teacher: That's going to be one thousand ten. This is a really hard number to write! Can I ask you something? How did you write nine thousand?

Maya: Nine-zero-zero-zero. Oh! Ten-zero-zero-zero.

Teacher: Try it. Let's see what it looks like. (*Maya writes* 10,000.)

Teacher: Nice! Now how would you write eleven thousand?

Maya: Eleven-zero-zero-zero.

Teacher: Now how about twelve thousand?

Maya: Twelve-zero-zero-zero.

Teacher: Now how about twelve thousand three hundred? (*Maya writes* 12,300. [*See Figure 3.4.*] *Ms. Morchower silently high-fives her and moves on to see what Alex is recording and to work with him on changing 12,003 to 12,300.*)

Figure 3.4
Maya figures out how to record the large quantities in her collection.

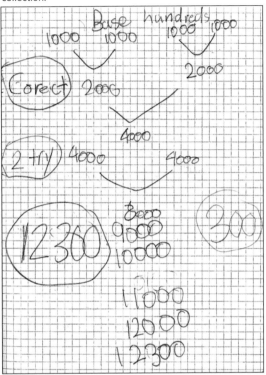

In this scenario, Maya has been given an authentic opportunity to learn to write numbers larger than she has written before. Her teacher has given her both the needed guidance and the space to figure it out on her own. By asking, "How did you write nine thousand?" Ms. Morchower gives Maya the chance to use what she knows (how to write 9,000) to figure out what she has not yet worked out and to apply it to writing numbers that cross into the ten thousands. This child was given the opportunity to construct meaning for herself.

Meanwhile, Alex, who was interested in taking a shortcut and not recording quite as diligently as Maya had ("You could just count this, and then it's a lot faster"), comes to see the shortcoming in his method. He may well be able to count up the piles of thousands as "1, 2, 3, . . . , 12," but applying his same method to the three extra hundred flats as "1, 2, 3" leaves him believing the total is "12,003." Ms. Morchower spends the next few minutes with him, asking where his recordings are and suggesting that written work can help us keep track of big numbers like these. Together, they retrace the steps the partners took to count their collection and write it down. Alex, too, writes 12,300 by the end of their time together.

Sara and Adrienne: Recordings That Match the Mathematics

In this scenario, the teacher has been thinking about how to make collection counting challenging for fifth graders. Ms. Fish wants them to be able to touch tangible items and to manipulate them but to be strategic about grouping them. She hopes the children will create systems for keeping track of what they have counted. She has heard from her colleagues next door that while the third- and fourth-grade students were getting to some big totals, they in general were struggling to create recordings that mathematically showed *how* they had counted. That seemed like something fifth graders could take on.

Ms. Fish presents Sara and Adrienne with the challenge of not just counting a collection of buttons but, rather, coming up with a total for the number of holes in a collection of mixed buttons. They are also tasked with making a corresponding recording that reflects how they did it. The girls cover a table and, when they run out of room, the floor around it as well, with groups of two-holed buttons, four-holed buttons, and no-holed buttons. They strategically decide to put four-holed buttons into groups of 5, and two-holed buttons into groups of 10, so that all of the groups have 20 holes in them. (See Figures 3.5 and 3.6.) Interestingly, when it comes time to count, they do not think of counting across the groups by 20s. Instead, they tackle each subcollection separately. They count up 43 buttons with four holes and multiply on paper to find 172 holes in that group. To count up the groups of two-holed buttons, they go back to the tangible, counting 32 piles by 10s (320) and then doubling that number to 640. Finally, they add their two figures together: $172 + 640 = 812$.

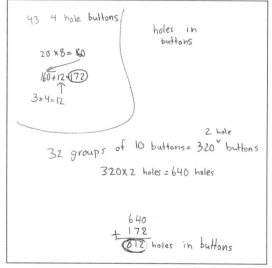

Figure 3.5
Keeping track of how many holes were in the collection of buttons.

Figure 3.6
Creating groups of buttons with 20 holes in each group.

The girls are asked to count features of objects—the buttonholes rather than the items themselves, the buttons. Even before they group them in any particular way, this already demands that Sara and Adrienne keep in mind two distinct sets at once. The holes cannot be manipulated or regrouped in the same way as the buttons.

The teacher observes that it is harder for the girls to keep track of the counted and not-counted piles of buttons than she expected. Like the younger students, recounting multiple times is part of the process. She notes that Sara and Adrienne persevere through the organizational challenge of managing the large number of items. They also keep good track of the addition and multiplication relationships they are using to successfully accomplish the task. And their number sentence shows in a straightforward way how many holes are in the four-holed buttons and how many holes are in the two-holed buttons (172 + 640). However, they do not find a way to record the number of two-holed buttons and the number of four-holed buttons in the collection or how many groups of each they had to make. This turns out to be a challenge they can successfully take up later in the year.

Sara and Adrienne at the End of Fifth Grade: Development over a School Year

In May, Ms. Fish returns to Counting Collections, believing there is more that she can extract from student recordings now that students have experienced both expressions and order of operations in the curriculum. She decides to revisit the students' work from September and ask them how their recordings might look at this point in the year. She brings pictures to the girls of the button counting they had completed in the fall and reminds them of what they had done and how. There is laughter when they remember how they had moved their button groups one at a time onto the floor as they counted, how hard it had been to keep track of all those groups, and how many times they had recounted.

The teacher then poses the following challenge. "Now that you've had pretty much your whole fifth-grade year, I want to see how you two have grown in the way you record and write about the collection that you counted." She asks them to write a number sentence that matches the organization of their previously counted collection. They are given only a photograph of their collection, not the items they had originally counted.

This is what they come up with: $8 \times 5 (+3) \times 4 + (32 \times 10) \times 2$. These numbers represent: 8 groups of 5 buttons, plus 3 extra buttons, all of which had 4 holes, plus 32 groups of 10 buttons, all of which had 2 holes. As the girls work, a problem for them arises in that they don't know how to make the "×4" apply to the entire set of four-holed buttons because they have already used parentheses to separate out the three extra buttons. Essentially, they are now dealing with how to record a fourth category of number, which is "the leftovers," or the three odd buttons. They know that group still needs to be multiplied by four, however, in order to find the total number of holes. So, they puzzle over how to make the "×4" apply to the whole number sentence.

Sara: It's like we need parentheses within parentheses, can we do that? (*She turns to Ms. Fish to look for a response. From some distance away, the teacher gives her a thumbs-up, and the girls continue for some time talking it out.*)

Adrienne: I think the "times 4" might have to be in the parentheses because . . .

Sara: No, I think it's the other side, you have to do the multiplying first, then you do the adding. So once you get both sides, you add it together. Remember? Adding is last.

Adrienne: Oh, yeah.

Teacher: So can I ask you to take a color (*indicating markers*) and show where the *holes* are represented in your equation. What part represents the holes?

Sara: The 8 × 5. Right?

Adrienne: No, I think it's the "times 4."

Teacher: I think different colors could help you see what you have. Why don't you try letting one color show the number of *groups* you have, one color show the number of buttons *in* a group, and one color the number of *holes*, whether that's two holes or four holes.

Sara: Do you want us to color everything?

Teacher: That seems like a good idea, because everything [you have recorded] represents something.

$$(8 \times 5 \,(+3) \times 4 + (32 \times 10) \times 2$$

- wholes in each button
- left over buttons
- #'s of buttons in a group
- # of groups

This teacher intervention is more directive than usual, which does accomplish the intended result: the girls are able to visualize the work they have already done. Ms. Fish then steps back to give them time and space to work things out, and the girls proceed for some time on their own. (See Figure 3.7.)

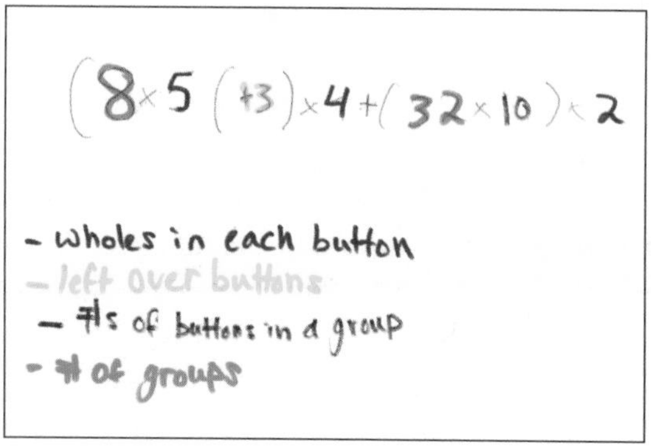

Figure 3.7
Sara and Adrienne annotate their notation for how many holes were in the buttons they counted.

Once the girls have color coded everything on their page, Ms. Fish returns and asks, "Do you want to know how mathematicians communicate that this whole group has four holes in it?" She then demonstrates at the board how to use brackets.

Teacher: You had eight groups of five buttons, right?
Girls: Yeah.
Teacher, (*writes on board* 8×5): You also had one extra group of three buttons, right?
Girls: Yeah.
Teacher, (*writes* $(8 \times 5) + 3$): So far, this is representing how many buttons there are, but we haven't represented that all of these buttons have four holes. One way mathematicians can communicate that *all* of these have four holes is by using brackets (*writes* $4[(8 \times 5) + 3]$).
Sara: Ooooooh! That's awesome!

The girls were provided with the information they needed at the optimal time. The instruction offered to them emerged from a real and pressing need. And the entire demonstration took roughly one minute.

To get the mathematicians to try their new skill out in a fresh context, Ms. Fish hands the girls a small bag of new buttons. The goal at this point for these capable students is clearly not to prove their counting competence but, rather, to practice a complex recording. Therefore, a small number in the collection suffices. The girls quickly count how many of each type of button they have and then never return to the physical piles. Instead, they use the color-coding system they had just been prompted by their teacher to use to keep track of exactly which numbers represented their *groups*, which numbers represented *the number of buttons in that group*, and which numbers represented *how many holes were in those buttons*. Extensive conversation ensued, as they worked to write a number sentence that matched the collection they now had, a number sentence that would get them to their total without even counting the buttons in their collection. (See Figure 3.8.)

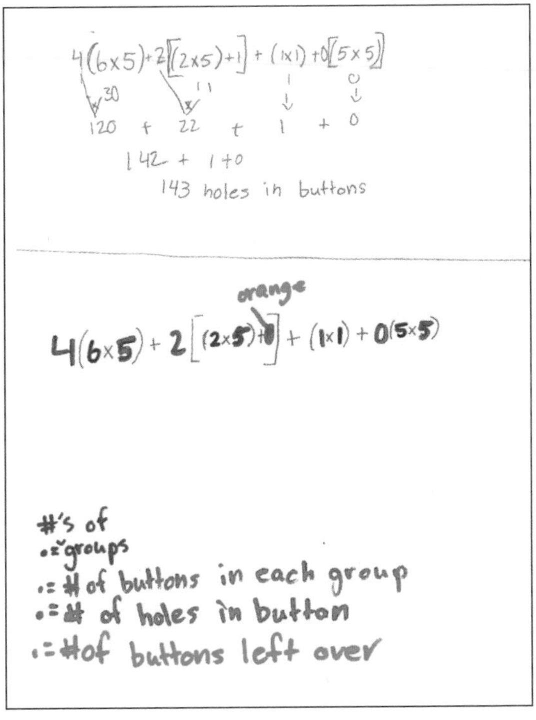

Figure 3.8
Sara and Adrienne using what they learned to write a number sentence for a new collection.

The straightforward explanation of the mathematical convention associated with brackets earlier in the morning made it possible for the girls to proceed with writing the following number sentence on a new collection of buttons.

The mathematics we see here beautifully represents the collection counted and is a significant step forward from their recording some months earlier. The girls are using the distributive and associative properties, and the appropriate formal notations for them, complete with brackets and parentheses, as a way to record a physical collection in front of them. Their knowledge of the order of operations also extends significantly beyond the ability to follow a prescribed set of rules to solve problems themselves. They are *using* those mathematical rules to *create* a number sentence that enables the mathematician who will make sense of their recording to follow the way they counted the collection. These girls are in the driver's seat.

Their teacher had faith that their struggle would be productive. She let it unfold and decided when to intervene. She also had the mathematical knowledge that was needed, ready in her pocket. Perfect timing cannot, of course, always happen, nor do we always have the ideal piece of information to offer. But as we become skilled kid-watchers and listeners, intrigued by the children's counting strategies and devoted to supporting them as they find ways to record their thinking, we can meet students where they are and help them take the next mathematical steps forward.

Teacher Decisions That Support Student Participation

So, how do we build classroom practice that makes this kind of mathematical work possible? Although it may seem contradictory, in a classroom devoted to children's thinking, teachers remain the greatest resource. While students count collections, a teacher makes several sets of key decisions that prove pivotal to the kind of work students can do. These decisions are related to setting up the physical environment and selecting collections, framing the tasks, establishing a safe emotional environment, helping students to form productive partnerships so they can effectively problem-solve as they work together, noticing what children are doing and asking questions about their work, simplifying and extending the tasks at hand based on students' needs, and deciding which conversations to bring back to the group that have the potential to enrich and extend what children can already do. Each of these takes skill and care on the part of the teacher. His or her intentional decisions contribute significantly to the growth of the students.

Setting Up the Environment: Getting Started

Even before students arrive, we carefully consider our classroom arrangements. There are places for collections to be stored and easily accessed by children, and there are comfortable places for children to work together at tables, in corners, and on the floor. This is as true for upper-grade classrooms as it is for primary grades, though the size of the furniture and its arrangement, as well as the content and size of the collections, will naturally change as children get older. There is a rug area or gathering place for the class to meet and storage areas where students will be able to independently access the collections, the tools available to them, and the math journals where they will record their work.

A teacher also selects and gathers appropriate and interesting collections for students to count. Some students will find collections for themselves in the classroom (tubs of books, classroom supplies), or bring them from home (eraser collections, Pokémon cards). But many collections the teacher will provide and display in interesting ways, perhaps in baskets or in mason jars. The teacher will look for objects from nature (shells), inexpensive items from discount stores (colored craft sticks), and objects from recycling centers (plastic bottle caps). Once oriented toward the value of these collections, families often contribute from home. So, the collections quickly accumulate and can be shared and traded with colleagues, to give children new and interesting materials to handle as the year progresses.

With the oldest and most capable students in elementary school, we seek to create complex collections of things to count, which might come in the form of packaged collections or collections with multiple features. We want students like Sara and Adrienne to have to work at mathematically recording collections with multiple parts or subsets. The collections might include buttons of different sizes, shapes, color, and number of holes; LEGOs with different numbers of studs and varying shapes and dimensions; dominoes of assorted colors and dots; shape and attribute links with different numbers of vertices and edges; mini animals with assorted numbers of legs, beaks, and so on; and coins of varying size, value, and color.

An Invitation to the Count

How might a teacher frame counting tasks in the upper grades? A straightforward starting point is to invite students to count collections in the same ways they have in the past. Their collections will contain larger numbers of items than before: 1,200 hair bands, 460 beads, 612 stickers. There will be higher expectations for the ways in which they will record their counting as well. Children are asked to show how they counted, what they counted, and what number they reached. Number sentences naturally emerge as one way to record. (See Figure 3.9.) For example, a collection of beads might be organized into 6 cups of 200 with 105 beads remaining and be recorded as $(6 \times 200) + 105 = 1,350$.

To encourage students to look at counting challenges in new ways, a teacher of older students might seek their buy-in by acknowledging the children's expertise. "I know you've been Counting Collections for your whole mathematical career, and you have a lot of experience with it. When you were younger, we might have asked you to count how many buttons were in this basket. Today, I am going to ask you to figure out how many holes are in the buttons. If you look closely, you'll notice they don't all have the same number of holes. You are also going to record what you found in your collection in a way that matches your process, so that someone who didn't watch you work could still retrace your steps."

Children will want new challenges, too. Teachers have found success in asking the class to take inventory of the supplies and books they will start the year with. The teacher might suggest that new packages of markers, for example, should not be opened and might pose the problem of counting unopened packages as inventory is taken. The counting of markers then involves figuring out how to count up by 8s or 12s (or working with the 12s as groups of 10s and 2s). Paper clips come in boxes of 125 or 200, and the boxes are shrink-wrapped together into quantities that stretch into the thousands. Classroom libraries sorted into tubs provide a complex challenge, as the numbers are unequal. An added challenge comes when the teacher stipulates that the books have been

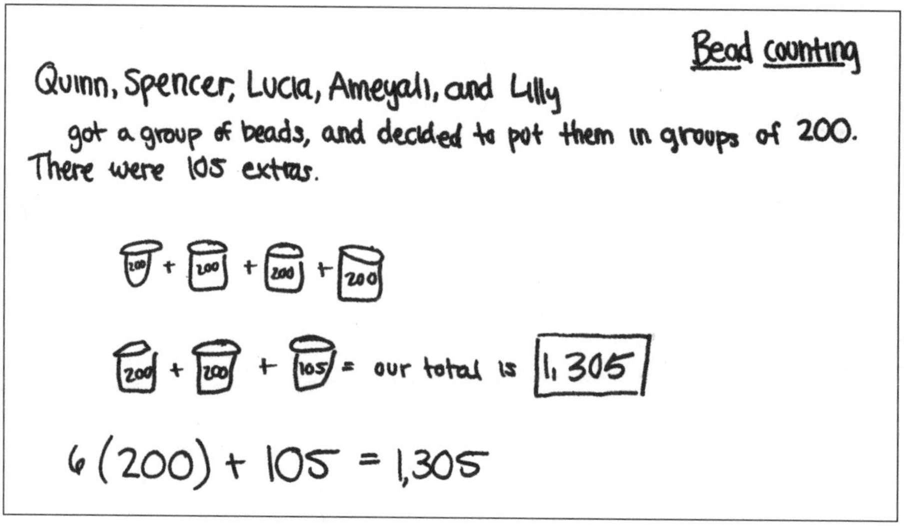

Figure 3.9
Counting and recording a collection of beads.

Figure 3.10
Recording so that
the notation
matches how the
collection was
counted.

carefully sorted and should not be mixed up. Big numbers will have to be written down and combined. (See Figure 3.10.)

Figure 3.11
Students capitalize on an opportunity to count discarded
pots after a major landscaping project at the school.

By inviting children to engage in a dialogue on the topic *What can we count?* students' ideas expand quickly. They notice that there are boxes awaiting delivery in the front office and wonder what's in them. Schools receive shipments regularly, and many things might be counted, such as crates of milk and cases of food coming into the cafeteria or school supplies coming into the office. Students can even invent systems to keep track of these shipments over time. It is interesting to find out how custodians and cafeteria workers go about that and to invite important people into our classrooms to share their work, expanding our mathematical communities. (See Figure 3.11.)

Early in the year, we want students to explore and get to know their schools, so we might send them out into their environment to discover how many cubbies there are in the entire school or how many tiles are in the hallway. It is not hard for children to find things to count in their homes and neighborhoods. This is an easy bridge to build between home

Figure 3.12
At first, as with younger students, children remain focused on getting to a total and simply labeling what they counted. Teachers will guide discussions around whether these initial recordings represent *how* the counting was accomplished and push for more complex and clearly labeled recordings.

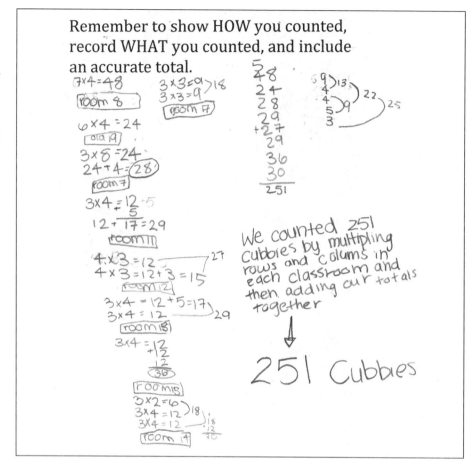

and school. Before you know it, students are counting everywhere they go. (See Figure 3.12.)

The Role of the Teacher

What does the teacher do while all this counting is going on? Primarily, he or she notices in detail what students are doing by listening actively to students' complete thoughts and strategies. In response to what he or she hears, the teacher becomes versatile and specific in the questions he or she asks. The teacher poses the following questions:

Tell me what you are doing. How you are counting this?
How will you record what you are doing?
I see you have already counted 250. How many do you think will be in the whole set?

How many 10s are in this whole collection?
Is there a way you can organize this so that someone can tell how many are
     here without counting?
How did you decide where to start?
How could you count this in a way that challenges you?
Is there a way to count these that might be more efficient?
What is working well for you as partners?
What will be your next step?

For experienced teachers, kid-watching and question-asking are well-developed skills. Experience allows a teacher to know what is unusual or interesting about what a child is doing, to notice the nuance of a child's strategy, and to be able to ask about it. Teachers new to Counting Collections can develop these skills, particularly with the support of a trusted coach or teaching partner. A teacher might consider having a colleague pull up a chair alongside him or her and record the questions he or she poses. Are there some questions that come naturally, that he or she is good at asking and falls back on frequently? Which ones were open ended? Which ones generated the most specific and interesting responses from students? Why might that have happened? What new question might the teacher want to try? A simple note card with that question written on it carried with the teacher as he or she travels through the math classroom the next day could serve as a prompt. Might there be an opening to try it out? In very little time, it becomes a part of the teacher's own natural repertoire.

Posing questions is a skill set like any other. We can absolutely get better at helping students articulate what they are doing and why. We can practice at asking questions that help children take pride in and ownership of their work and questions that extend or refine what they are doing by giving them the chance to talk their thinking through. We have the chance to practice asking questions every day, questions that communicate to children that we see, get, and marvel at the hard work they are doing.

Conferring: Noticing What Students Need and Responding

Beyond asking questions, a teacher confers with students. Just as in the primary grades, these targeted conversations in the upper grades build on what the teacher has noticed. There are many possible topics for these conferences. Given the large number of objects in a student's collection and time considerations, how is he or she tackling this collection efficiently? Has someone else in the class tried an organizational strategy that may be helpful? Given the importance of accuracy, is everything accounted for? What happens when students count twice but get two different results? Does the representation match the actions taken and the ways in which the materials were organized? How is the partnership going? How have students extended themselves and made their work challenging?

The goal of conferring is to help students articulate what they are doing, consider how it is working for them, and possibly refine or extend their strategy in a way that builds on what they already can do.

For teachers who have the vantage point of seeing what is happening throughout the classroom, patterns emerge. After noticing that they are repeating the same conversation with several different students, they recognize that a conversation about this topic may benefit the whole class. For example, if they notice a great deal of recounting going on, they might pose the question of how we can avoid starting from scratch every time we lose track or get distracted. Back in a class debrief, students often come up with helpful suggestions for their peers.

Conferring: Timing and Teaching with a Light Touch

The challenge for teachers is often that we are so good at what we do. We are paid to teach, after all. Holding back, listening carefully, and not jumping in to demonstrate to children what can be done to solve the very compelling counting challenges we have created for them can pose a challenge to *us*, as teachers. It takes an abiding faith in the constructivist nature of learning to be a listener first and, only then, to tailor our conversations with students to what they are teaching us they can do and what they may need next. When the child can discover and create new knowledge for himself, out of a need to replace an old way of thinking with a new one, learning is integrated. The new skill or strategy can be accessed and tried again.

Consider the following scenario from a third-grade classroom and the role the teacher plays. Especially important is her decision to step back.

Michael and William are counting a collection of colorful tiles. After some trial and error, they decide that 15 tiles should go into each Dixie cup because that is the number that seems to fit best. They have filled well over 30 cups with this large collection! While William is pulled away from the classroom, the teacher watches over Michael's shoulder as he attempts to figure out how many tiles there are in total. She observes him using the following strategy: pick up one filled cup and move it to the other side, write the number *15*, move another filled cup, write *30*, move another cup, write *45*, and so on. Although Michael writes those first few numbers quickly, it is taking him some time to figure out the next number in this counting-by-15s sequence.

He perseveres, though, and with the numbers 15, 30, 45, 60, 75, 90, 105, 120, 135, 150 written on his paper (corresponding to the 10 cups of 15 that he has already counted), the teacher notices an opportunity to chat with Michael and possibly offer a suggestion. She first prompts Michael to explain what he had done so far, and Michael tells the teacher about making cups of 15 and having to go up by 15s on his paper. Then, the teacher invites Michael to notice something about what he has already done.

Teacher, (*gesturing over the 10 cups that Michael has already counted*)**:** Michael, how many cups did you count already here?

Michael, (*hesitates, then begins to count the 10 cups*)**:** Umm . . . 10.

Teacher: Right, you've counted 10 cups. And how many tiles was that?

Michael, (*hesitates, looking at the cups, then looking at his paper*)**:** Umm . . . 150.

Teacher: So 10 cups made 150. What do you think would happen if we made another group of 10 cups over here (*gesturing over the uncounted cups*)?

Michael: Umm . . .

Teacher: How many tiles would there be in these 10 cups (*continuing to gesture over the uncounted cups*)?

Michael: Umm . . . two hund . . . (*trails off*)

Teacher: Just these 10 cups, not all of them together.

Michael: Umm . . .

During this interaction, the teacher took the opportunity to intervene when Michael had counted 10 cups of 15 and knew it was 150. Anticipating that his strategy would become too cumbersome as he still had many more cups of tiles remaining, she hoped that he might consider another group of 150 rather than continuing to increment by 15s. By highlighting that he had already created a group of 150, the teacher was attempting to help Michael notice an idea that was mathematically interesting and connected to what he already knew. However, as evidenced by Michael's hesitant responses, this idea did not make sense to him.

The teacher's intervention has not helped Michael move forward this time. We are familiar with this moment. The student has not made sense of the strategy offered, one that was suggested by the teacher. We have found that the best way out sometimes is to backtrack to help students find solid ground again. The teacher says, "You know what, you had a good strategy going for you, and I'm trying to move you in a different direction. Keep doing what you're doing!"

Representation of Student Ideas

In addition to developing relationships with increasingly large numbers and efficient systems for managing those quantities, the big area of growth we want to push on with older students is around accurate recording. In working with middle-grade students on Counting Collections, we initially notice that the students return to counting into piles of "counted" and "uncounted" objects. They work at getting a total of the large group and not necessarily on the organization of the objects. This kind of counting does not necessarily lend itself to the more complex recordings we want to set in motion, like those that Adrienne and Sara tackled when they counted buttonholes. So what steps can we take to nudge the recordings forward?

To prompt organization around a large number, teachers might say, "As you work, I want to be able to see how many are there and how you've organized your collection, just by looking at your table. When you are ready, let me know, and I will take a picture of it." In this way, the teacher is not suggesting that children organize in any particular way (by 10s or 20s or 2s, etc.). Children still invent the way they will count, but they are prompted to think about the third-party viewer. In the same way that writers at this age begin to consider their audience and can give some thought to how their writing will "read" to someone else, mathematicians too need to work at communicating to other mathematicians, and at considering how an outsider might be able to understand their work.

Heightened accountability for the physical organization of collections at tables is the starting point that spurs the next step: recording the collection in a way that matches the mathematician's process. In Figure 3.13, we see one third-grade student's organization of a collection of sharks' teeth. Cassius chose to count by 20s and created these arrays without any specific prompt. As promised, the teacher snapped a photo that could be used for further discussion.

The photo caught the attention of other teachers. It started at a math planning meeting. Knowing what was coming up in the math curriculum within the next month, teachers were excited about the arrays evident in Cassius's photo, specifically that there were 5-by-4 arrays evident within the larger 3-by-4 array. In no time, this photo had gone back to other classrooms, and students across several different grades were using the image to practice their recording skills. (See Figures 3.14–3.15.)

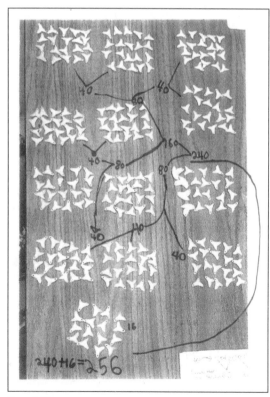

Figure 3.13
One student counted and regrouped the numbers in a way that made sense to him to simply get a total.

Figure 3.14
A second student tried recording in a way that more closely mirrored what was on the table by adding groups of 20s, three at a time.

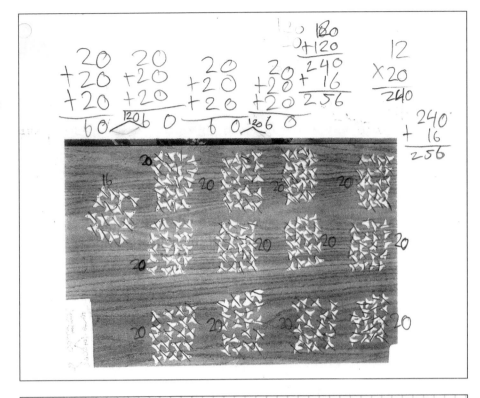

Figure 3.15
A third student, Jingjing, tried to represent the arrays with numbers in exactly the way that the collection had been organized, transferring her work to a graph paper. She even recognized that the extra group on the bottom was only a 4-by-4 array and needed to be added separately.

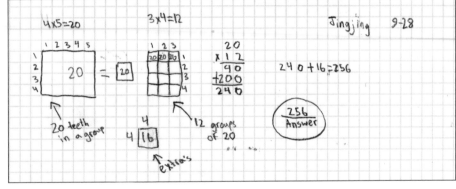

Creating Opportunities to Practice Specific Skills

How can teachers explicitly build skills around recording? Sometimes having students practice recording using someone else's work can be helpful. For example, Ms. Phillips noticed that several fourth-grade students were not recording their counting in ways that authentically matched their process, because they were more focused on reaching the total. To provide them some peer models to look to, she took pictures of some of the collections they were counting and presented them to her former students in the fifth-grade class next-door (see Figure 3.16). She knew that they had developed more expertise with recording and that her class would benefit from the peer modeling. She also wanted to use student models rather than showing her own way of recording.

Ms. Phillips asked the fifth graders to see whether they could make sense of how the fourth graders' collections had been counted based on photos alone. They then were tasked with clearly labeling each part of the collection in the photo by writing directly on the images and recording a number sentence that would provide a total. This exercise helped the older students understand what it meant to match a recording to a collection and to practice at it, all in the name of modeling or helping their younger peers. It improved their own skills when they recorded their own collections. And when Ms. Phillips returned to her fourth-grade classroom to share the work, the younger students had some interesting models to evaluate. There was both agreement and disagreement about whether the recordings matched the counting well, and rich conversations ensued, both for the students and for teachers from several classrooms who had recordings to compare and analyze together.

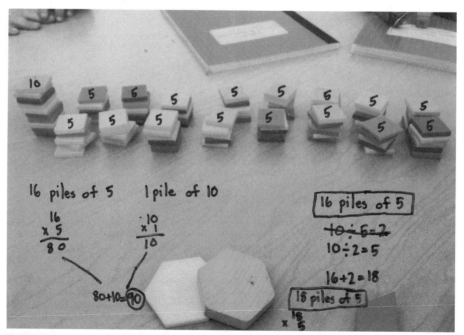

Figure 3.16
Children analyzed photos taken in another classroom and wrote directly on the printed photographs. The exercise was meant to give students practice at recording how a collection had been counted.

Supporting Students in Working Together: Social Development and Mathematical Communication Go Hand in Hand

Research informs us that it matters a great deal that children engage with one another's mathematical ideas. As teachers, we know that the social skills students draw on to collaborate with their classmates take time to develop. The practice of Counting Collections layers social demands onto cognitive ones, providing a context in which both rich mathematical work and social development can happen. Although the math is important, the opportunity early in the school year to establish relationships between young colleagues who will work together all year is invaluable, too. If we mean to create classroom communities devoted to equity and respect, there are no shortcuts. Having students work in partnerships and small groups to get to know one another, to communicate with one another about logistics (*Where should we work today?*) and choices of materials (*What should we count?*), and to work through the different ways they inevitably approach and organize the tasks, all provide opportunities for social growth. Further, we have evidence that when children work together, the work that children can do changes *mathematically*. The children require one another to become better mathematicians. Consider the following interaction.

Octavio and Darrius chose to sort their Unifix cubes by color and to add up each color group (see Figure 3.17). They worked together successfully to count

Figure 3.17
Blocks are organized by color and left in piles.

and label how many cubes were in each color group. Independently, they then took on the task of recording and adding those numbers to gather the total. They came up with different answers, and one of the boys immediately said, "Wait, you're wrong." Being competitive fourth-grade boys, they wanted to be fast, to be finished first, and to be right.

They went back to the blocks to find out what the "real total" was supposed to be. First, they efficiently verified that they had written down the correct numbers for each group.

Octavio: Brown.
Darrius: 47!
Octavio: Maroon.
Darrius: 69!
Darrius: Red.
Octavio: 29!

In the course of their rechecking, the teacher, Ms. Viera, announced to the entire class that she wanted to "be able to take a photo of your collection and just by looking at it, know how many are in each group." So, the boys reorganized the blocks not into piles but into sticks of 10 and labeled their totals in a more organized way. They came to agreement that there were 297 blocks, a total they were now reaching for the first time.

When they then revisited their recordings, they were surprised that, as confident as they had been that the other boy had been wrong, that *neither* of them had the accurate total of 297. Octavio had recorded 287, and Darrius had recorded 268. This was the moment when the teacher came by to encourage the boys to find the error in both pieces of work. In the end, they discovered that one boy had omitted the red group entirely from this total, and the other made a regrouping mistake when combining two color groups. Both boys found both errors together, and they were proud of themselves that they had done so.

Working independently, Octavio and Darrius would not have known they had made the mistake to begin with. The problem arose because their answers were different. And the actions they took as a result of that discrepancy prompted them to fine-tune their mathematical thinking. First, they developed a fast and efficient system of cross-checking. Next, they had to up their game regarding organization of their collection, which had been organized "quick and dirty" the first time by color. Third, they had an authentic opportunity to focus on accuracy in both method and answer, which would not have arisen had they worked alone. Fourth, they were proud of themselves, and they eagerly went back to their teacher to show her that they had found their errors. This gave them the added mathematical benefit of summarizing and articulating their process one last time. Finally, being fast, competitive boys, they raced to clean up their blocks and try to be the first ones finished. As they broke up their 10s, they shot them basketball style one at a time back into the small wooden crate they had come from and called it a day. They had fun.

Of course, problems sometimes arise when students work together. There will be disagreements, and teachers will spend time helping students untangle feelings, come to understand each other's ideas, share materials, and work equitably. Truthfully, there are days when we feel reluctant to take all of this on. It's hard. It takes time. It would be nice to have days when we could just teach math! Alas, we teach children. And, so, we remind ourselves of what we know to be true: the social conflicts that come up present real learning opportunities for children. When we add to this that there are great benefits mathematically to student collaboration and that students often accomplish together what they cannot accomplish alone, we are willing once again to invest our time and energy in supporting student problem solving on both fronts.

Sequencing Tasks to Build Mathematical Ideas Across the Year

How might we expect counting concepts to develop across a year, and how can we plan for multiple entry points for students?

At the beginning of the year, the pattern we have seen across classrooms is that counting work is largely related to number sense. Students are grouping things in ways that continue to build place value understanding. They are comparing quantities and developing relationships with those numbers. They are learning to record in ways that make sense to others. They are learning to make sense of others' recordings, too. They are working at creating organizational systems that increase efficiency for large collections. They are using multiplicative reasoning as they group items. Sometimes they are organizing the same collection in two different ways. They are building working relationships with one another. They are building confidence and a sense of agency in their classroom. And students are excited about math.

Consider how to provide multiple entry points for students even early in the year. One way to increase complexity for students is to see whether they can find ways to count things that can't be moved. Students eagerly take up the challenge of trying to count the bricks that line the walkway to the office or the number of cubbies in the school. When objects cannot be manipulated and grouped, the challenge increases.

Different Types of Collections That Children Count

- Loose and single objects that can be moved around and grouped in any way that makes sense to the child (e.g., a basket of markers)
- Fixed, small collections of items that can't be moved (e.g., panes of glass in windows)
- Collections that come in packages that can't be opened but which can be moved (e.g., twelve markers in a box, with multiple sets to count)
- Larger collections of fixed items that can't be moved (e.g., the books on the shelves of the library or the number of student cubbies in the building)
- Collections with multiple attributes to keep track of (e.g., LEGOs with different numbers of studs)

Consider the following scenario. Gen and Aryana went with their class on a community counting walk. In the neighborhood, they found a window made of 14 rows of 6 circular pieces of glass. Aryana immediately saw the window as organized into 6 columns with 14 panes in each. She ultimately recorded $(1 \times 14) + (1 \times 14) + (1 \times 14) + (1 \times 14) + (1 \times 14) + (1 \times 14)$. She then worked to multiply 6×14. Her partner Gen could count by 5s. She circled groups of five horizontally, counted them up, and then added on the remaining column of 14 by counting on by 1s. She had counted the windowpanes as $(14 \times 5) + 14$.

Back in the classroom, they used a photo from their field trip to record the unique ways they had seen the same thing. This was harder than counting discrete objects. They had to find a way to be able to work with the fixed windowpanes they had seen. Printing a photo for them allowed them to "touch" and count, if not move the groups in ways they might have preferred.

Working with Complex Collections

As the year progresses, the collections that middle- and upper-grade students work with may get smaller rather than larger, so that they can try more complex recordings and put to use their emerging understanding of mathematical properties as they record. These third graders found a systematic way to keep track of how many of each type of domino they had and used an impressive amount of multiplication and incremental addition to reach a grand total of 162 dots. For example, in the side margin the "21" represents one domino with eleven dots and five dominoes with two dots, which could be numerically written as $(1 \times 11) + (5 \times 2)$. In this math hour, they completed six such equations, and then the addition of those six figures together. They also wrote a complete number sentence representing each type of domino in their collection at the bottom of the page: $3 + 11 + 10 + 16 + 20 + 24 + 14 + 12 + 6 + 16 + 26 = 162$ and added the numbers together incrementally. Can you find the two errors that affect their accuracy? (See Figure 3.18.)

A fourth grader first sorted her LEGOs by the number of studs on each block. Then, she carefully recorded what she had by drawing each LEGO. However, it was taking some time, so she started using numbers ("8") to represent the studs. Then, she totaled the value of all the studs to reach 193. Finally, she created a single, correct, and accurate number sentence using multiplication to represent how many of each type of block she had: $(7 \times 1) + (9 \times 2) + (11 \times 4) + (14 \times 8) + (1 \times 12) = 193$.

We have seen upper-grade students even conceive of collections as having fractional parts. In Figure 3.19, we see work from fourth-grade partners who decided that a sixteen-stud LEGO would represent one whole and agreed that every "peg" on every block in their mixed collection of LEGOs needed to be represented in the equation. They created a table and worked to figure out how many "wholes" there were through their number sentence. These students certainly figured out how to make the familiar task of Counting Collections into a unique and very challenging experience for themselves. (See Figure 3.19.)

The counting challenge another child set for himself was to build a LEGO structure and to keep track of the number of studs in the LEGOs of varying dimensions he used for his structure. He ended up recording fifteen separate multiplication equations to represent all of the different types of LEGOs he used and

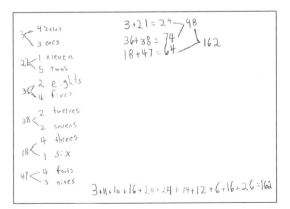

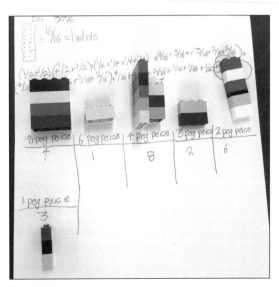

Figure 3.18
Figuring out how many dots are on a collection of dominoes.

Figure 3.19
Working with fractions in counting LEGOs.

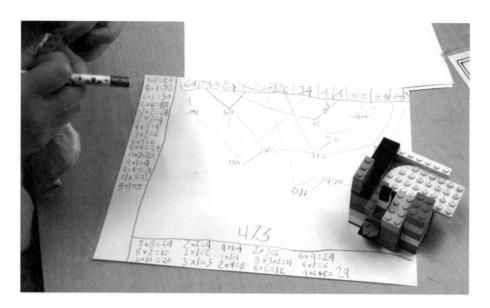

then regrouping those fifteen numbers until he reached the total of 473. That's a lot of math squeezed out of one LEGO creation. (See Figure 3.20.)

All of these opportunities provide extensions for our upper-grade counters, stretching students well beyond a straightforward count of single items. We encourage you to keep innovating and sharing your ideas with others (see Appendix 3).

Organizing Very Large Numbers

A different way to add complexity is to ask students to organize a collection of very large numbers. In one fifth-grade classroom, Ms. Kern asked students to represent the number 10,000 and provided objects like beans, tiny rubber bands, birdseeds, and sequins. How could these items be organized to show that number? What might best help younger students looking at our posters understand "what is inside" of the number 10,000? And if you run short and have fewer than 10,000 items available, how might you be able to abstractly show the number anyway? If we were representing 10,000 grains of rice, would it be adequate to count out the first 1,000 grains and then approximate the next nine groups by creating groups of similar size? If so, how might we change how we report out our results?

For those students ready for an extra challenge, it is easy to cross into more abstract problem solving around our chosen number: *How many baggies holding 100 rubber bands each would we need to hold 10,000 rubber bands? Given*

Figure 3.21
Students work on
the challenge of
representing 10,000
objects.

the average length of a line of 100 beans, how far would 10,000 beans stretch? If we have 75 cups to hold paper clips, and we find that we can fit 125 paper clips into each cup, will we have enough cups to contain 10,000 paper clips? (See Figure 3.21.) Students can also help create the problems that interest them.

Counting That Leads to Problem Solving

In the same way that readers learn to select just-right books, young mathematicians learn how to set just-right challenges for themselves. When counting by 10s and 20s is easy, we have seen students count items into cups of 19s. If getting a total for five packs of markers with 12 markers in each can quickly be counted, a mathematician can extend the problem for herself: *How many would be in 10 packs or 30 packs?* When a child discovers that a beaded necklace has 75 beads per strand, could he figure out a way to count a fistful of strands that vary slightly in length? In these ways, children with strong counting skills and number sense find ample challenge crossing over into the world of problem solving.

A student can be given the task, for example, of figuring out how many pens would be in a pack if a package of 18 and a package of 24 are wrapped together, and if twelve such packages are sold in a case. A further part of the challenge might involve finding out what a *pallet* is and picturing how items are delivered and displayed at a box store such as Costco. If 15 cases of markers are sold on a pallet, how many colored pens would be on a complete pallet? A problem like this offers a lot of opportunity for extending Counting Collections to a problem-solving scenario.

Asking Children to Reflect on Their Process

Another challenge that our upper elementary students can benefit from is the chance to reflect, either verbally or in writing, on their own growth. To return to fifth graders Sara and Adrienne, our now-famous buttonhole counters, we asked the girls to think about their process at the end of the day.

Adrienne said, "It really helped us to learn about the bracket today. If we hadn't thought of that we wouldn't have gotten to this part. We had to incorporate a lot of the steps that we did into one number sentence. Before, we kept trying a lot of different ways to write a number sentence, but with the brackets, it was easier because then we knew how to use them the right way and we understood them very well. It helped us match what we were trying to figure out."

They also were asked to compare their early-year recording with their end-of-year recording and to reflect on their own growth.

Sara reflected, "Last time our only goal was to find the answer to the problem, but this time, we were trying to justify our answer that made mathematical sense and in a way that would let other mathematicians trace our work. The big difference was that this time, we were trying to make it so that other people could understand instantly what we did. I used to rely on what I saw to help me find the answer, but I didn't always know how to show how I got my answer."

Being asked to count a collection provided them the context for doing all of this mathematics. And being asked about their process helped them articulate their own growth. Not only can we appreciate and take pride in the evolution of the girls' counting skills across the year, but more importantly, they can as well.

Counting Matters

We won't deny it. Classrooms engaged in Counting Collections can be messy, and they are not quiet places. We cannot foresee all of the mathematics that will unfold. Conflicts arise that have to be worked through. We invite you to take the risk anyway. Collection counting classrooms are joyful and productive places, matching the tone and energy level we strive for in classrooms devoted to preadolescents. Children grow as friends and colleagues as they work together. They become more skilled organizers, communicators, compromisers, and problem solvers. Mathematically speaking, Counting Collections offers multiple points of entry for those children deepening number sense and for those extending into complex recordings. When we create opportunities to count in the upper grades, we are building a spiral curriculum, giving children important opportunities to build on their foundational experiences in the primary grades. In creating a common activity across our kindergarten through fifth-grade classrooms, we offer children something familiar so that they can experience success and continuity in their learning. We give children the gift of time to circle back and to have the satisfaction of having counted fully and well across all of their elementary years.

We are excited to develop further our own practice as teachers, because we see endless opportunities for us to draw on the mathematics the children keep bringing back to us when we allow them to count. We don't know all the specifics that will arise ahead of time and that makes the undertaking a leap of faith. It is one well worth taking. The children's work gives us so much to talk about and share as colleagues, too, extending our professional collaboration across grade levels and schools.

We wish you every success, and we look forward to hearing about and learning from your journey into Counting Collections with your third, fourth, and fifth graders!

Reference

Goldstone, Bruce. 2010. *Great Estimations.* New York: Henry Holt.

CHAPTER 4

Choral Counting K–2

by Lynsey Gibbons and
Kassia Omohundro Wedekind

Choral Counting and the Community of Mathematicians

On a January morning, Mrs. Olson gathers her students on the carpet in the front of their classroom. "Let me tell you something really interesting that I've noticed recently about our class of mathematicians," she begins, signaling to her first graders that they are mathematical thinkers with ideas worthy of her interest and curiosity.

"I've noticed that many of you are interested in big numbers. Just yesterday, I saw Rashad and Denia reading *How Many Jellybeans?* Remember when they showed us what 1,000 jellybeans looks like?" Students responded saying that was a lot of jellybeans. Mrs. Olson continued, "And many of you have been interested in how we can count collections when there's a lot of something, right? Yesterday Brandon and Nathalia showed us how they organized that big collection of pom-poms. How many pom-poms were there, Nathalia?" asks Mrs. Olson.

"134," Nathalia replies, beaming with pride.

"134! That's a lot!" confirms Mrs. Olson. "Many of you are interested in what happens when we count *past* 100. Today in our choral count we'll be *starting* with a number less than 100, but we won't stop at 100. We'll keep going and going and see what happens with the numbers. I know you all are curious about these numbers, and I am curious to see what you notice about these numbers."

The first graders are smiling and intrigued. Choral Counting builds on children's natural curiosity around counting and numbers. Mrs. Olson has chosen this count because she knows it is important for her students to notice patterns

77

in three-digit numbers and extend their understanding of place value past 100 but also because she wants to respond to an interest in larger quantities coming from her class. Although she knows that not all of her students can count independently past 100, they are collectively capable of doing so through counting chorally. And whether or not they are independent with this counting sequence yet, Mrs. Olson knows that they will benefit from talking about what they notice in the written record of the count with their peers.

Mrs. Olson leads the class in the count, beginning at 92 and pausing the count when they get to 135. "Look how far we've counted! Look what some of those numbers in the hundreds look like! I wonder what you all are noticing about these numbers. Let's have thirty seconds to think about it quietly. I'll let you know when it is time to turn to your partner to share your ideas." (See Figure 4.1.)

After a few minutes of thinking and sharing with partners, Mrs. Olson brings the class back together. The class shares various noticings and patterns they have seen. After a pause in the conversation, Mrs. Olson decides to return to an idea she heard shared during the turn-and-talk. "I heard Gabby say something, and I'm wondering what you all think of her idea. Would you share what you noticed, Gabby?"

At the beginning of the year, Gabby was hesitant about sharing her thinking, often responding, "I don't know" or "I don't think I'm right" when invited to share. However, Choral Counting is a place Gabby seems more ready to jump in to respond to Mrs. Olson's inviting question, "What do you notice?"

Figure 4.1
Mrs. Olson records what her class notices on the 92 to 135 count by 1s.

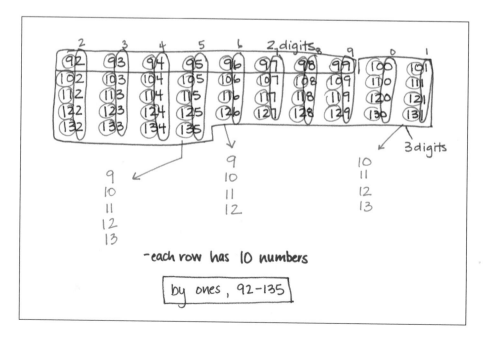

"I saw that just a few numbers—eight numbers—have two numbers in them. The rest of them—all those other numbers in the rest of the row and the other rows—they all have three numbers," responded Gabby.

"Did you all see that, too?" Mrs. Olson asks the class as she uses purple marker to mark the numbers to which Gabby refers. "Only these numbers [gesturing to 92–99] have two digits and all the rest [gesturing to the other numbers on the chart] have three digits. I'm really wondering about Gabby's idea. What happens after 99 when we're counting? Why do we have three digits after that? Let's talk to our partners again about Gabby's idea."

Choral Counting in the Primary Grades

Choral Counting gets to the heart of what we want for our mathematical communities. This activity creates space for all students to notice, to wonder, and to pursue interesting ideas. Students and teachers alike wonder together about patterns, and why and how numbers change or stay the same. Choral Counting also allows teachers like Mrs. Olson to be curious about students' thinking, elicit and listen deeply to their ideas, and consider next steps for their development as mathematical thinkers.

Perhaps most important, Choral Counting is an opportunity to engage in joyful mathematics! In this space, we wonder and take up ideas that are interesting to the community of mathematicians. Choral Counting is a space for children and their teachers to playfully engage in the work of constructing important mathematical ideas and to lay the foundation for mathematical thinking both within the walls of their classrooms and beyond.

Choral Counting capitalizes on young children's interest in numbers. In the primary classroom, Choral Counting provides opportunities for children to reason, to predict, and to justify as they notice what happens to numbers as they count together. Recording the count also enables children to readily ask questions and notice patterns that emerge in their counting.

"What do you think will come next? How do you know?"
"If we continue with this count, will we ever say the number 75?"
"Wow, look at all those fives!"
"The numbers are going 5 then zero then 5 then zero."

Counting aloud together is a common practice in many primary classrooms. However, the strategic recording and facilitating of a conversation around mathematical ideas may be newer adaptations of this important activity. This

instructional activity is a powerful tool for teachers of all levels and experiences
in that it has a predictable structure yet allows for flexibility and innovation.

Big Mathematical Ideas: Beginning Counting and Number Sense

There is much to learn about early number that will help build young students'
ideas and mathematical ability. Young students need lots of opportunities to
work on their knowledge of number. There are three aspects of number that
students have to coordinate: (1) the number word, (2) the symbolic notation,
and (3) the quantity (see Figure 4.2). Number words are the words assigned to
each number. For example, *three* is said to represent the number 3, which represents this quantity.

Choral Counting is a great way to help young students work on developing
their understanding of number. This activity also helps students to coordinate
the number word with the symbolic notation, as the teacher records the count
where all students can see.

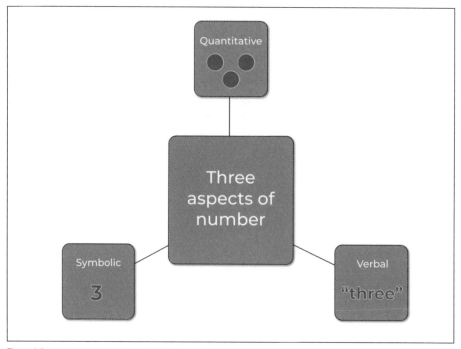

Figure 4.2
Three aspects of number.

Figure 4.3
Young children explore many aspects of number through Choral Counting.

Young students need to learn to count forward in order to be able to recall the number word that comes directly before or directly after a number. Choral counts can help young students to learn the sequence as they count aloud together, first by ones and later by other increments typically included in the primary grades such as 10s, 5s, and 2s. (See Figure 4.3.) But we do not want to limit children to only these increments. As we show in this chapter, because we record the count and discuss with children what they notice, a count by 10s can also include within it, counting by 100s or 50s, depending on how you choose to record the count. Although there is not much research on backward counting and we do not view it as an important priority in the primary grades, Choral Counting can open up a playful look at what happens as we count backward. And teachers may find it useful to connect strategically selected backward counts in second grade to students' developing repertoire of subtraction strategies.

Some early number ideas that can be explored and extended through Choral Counting with kindergarten through second graders:

- **The counting sequence**
  This is the order in which we say the numbers ("1, 2, 3, 4, . . ."). While we take it for granted that 15 comes immediately after 14 when counting forward by 1s, young children may still be in the process of constructing this understanding. If you ask students, "What comes right after or right before 14?" some young children will need to go back to one and count forward to figure this out. Children may easily know that 24 comes immediately after 23 but may stumble with knowing that 40 comes right after 39.

- **Coordinating the number word with the written symbol**
  Students learn to coordinate the number word with the symbolic notation (e.g., *three* is written like 3).

- **Thinking about relative size and quantity**
  How much does a number represent? How far away is it from other numbers? After counting by 5s to 60 and 2s to 60, students might notice

that it takes many fewer counts to reach 60 by 5s and discuss some ideas about what this means about the relative size of the numbers we are counting by. They may also make a connection to their Counting Collections and how they choose to group them (i.e., "When I made groups of 2, I had a lot more groups than when I combined the 2s into groups of 10").

- **Developing place value understanding**
  Understanding place value occurs by exploring patterns that ground our base 10 number system and allows us to more easily figure out what number comes next. We will explore a few of the many patterns in our base 10 number system in this chapter. Students will rely on knowledge of these patterns to figure out what number comes next in a count (e.g., I know that there are ten numbers in the 20s when I say, "20, 21, 22, . . .").
- **Skip-counting**
  Skip-count by 2s, 3s, 4s, 5s, 10s, 20s, 25s, 50s, as well as a range of other increments. Going up and down whole numbers by different increments will give students opportunities to explore aspects of structure of our number system in ways that could benefit their computational work and their understanding of how numbers are related to one another.
- **Patterns and features of number**
  Students will notice and talk about many patterns as they study their class counts. In counting by 5s, they might notice alternating even and odd numbers, while in counting by 2s, they might notice all the numbers are even. In counting by 4s, students might notice that the ones digit repeats in a particular sequence 4, 8, 2, 6, 0. They may use these patterns to determine whether a number could appear in the count and where. They may think about why these patterns occur.

Let's dig into how we can work on some of these big mathematical ideas within Choral Counting in the primary grades. We'll take you to three class-rooms where we will explore Choral Counting, and, at the end, we'll provide a table for some additional counts to give you ideas that can help your students as they develop their ability to count and develop number sense.

Getting Started with Choral Counting

Let's begin by considering counting by 1s, each time recording it in a few different ways. Pick up a pencil and take a look at the examples that follow. Notice and mark the patterns you see. How do the different recordings highlight certain ideas over others?

Recording A

1	2	3	4	5	6	7	8	9	10
11	12	13	14	15	16	17	18	19	20
21	22	23	24	25	26	27	28	29	30
31	32	33	34	35	36	37	38	39	40

Recording B

1	6	11	16	21	26	31	36
2	7	12	17	22	27	32	37
3	8	13	18	23	28	33	38
4	9	14	19	24	29	34	39
5	10	15	20	25	30	35	40

Recording C

1	2	3	4
5	6	7	8
9	10	11	12
13	14	15	16
17	18	19	20
21	22	23	24
25	26	27	28
29	30	31	32
33	34	35	36
37	38	39	40

While the counts are identical, students may notice and want to talk about different ideas as a result of how the count has been recorded. Recording A resembles the familiar hundred chart. Using formal or informal language, students may look down a column to notice that the digit in the ones place stays the same or may notice that a jump down in the column is a jump of 10. Students often comment, "It goes 7, 7, 7, 7 . . . " In Recording B, students may notice jumps of five going across a row. They also may notice that two columns of five numbers make up a group of 10 and begin to think about the number of 5s and 10s in 40. In Recording C, students may notice other patterns in the ones place looking down a column or how often the tens place changes in the rows. While you may have ideas about what you would like to highlight when you decide how you will record the count, the joy of Choral Counting comes from hearing the unexpected ideas from students and pursuing students' thoughts and wonders.

Thinking ahead to how a count will be recorded is one of the most important parts of planning a choral count. As you plan a choral count, try recording the count in several different ways in the planning template or your own notebook. Or use our online planning tool to help you easily create different displays of a count (see sten.pub/choralcounting). Mark what you think students will notice using a variety of colors. Think about what students might notice given different ways of recording their count. Think also about whether there are particular mathematical ideas you hope to pursue.

When planning a count consider these questions:

- Should I record this count horizontally in rows or vertically in columns?
- How many numbers should I record in each row or column?
- With which number should I start and end my count?
- How many numbers do we need to count in order for students to notice patterns?

In some cases, there is value in recording the same or similar counts in different ways in order to draw out different ideas from students. For example, you could record a similar count, counting by 10s off the decade, in different ways. One day you may count by 10s, starting at 4 and record horizontally writing 10 numbers in each row. Later in the week you may count by 10s, starting at 26 and record vertically. Giving students multiple opportunities to notice patterns and consider ideas is part of the power of the Choral Counting routine (see Appendix 2 for planning sheets).

Counting by 1s with Kindergartners

Kindergartners enter school with a wide range of prior mathematical experiences. Teachers may wonder, *Are all of my students ready for Choral Counting?* One of the beauties of Choral Counting is that it offers all students opportunities to contribute to discussions and grow mathematical ideas. Let's take a look into Ms. Pierce's kindergarten class in November in which students have been learning how to notice patterns and talk to one another about their thinking.

As she plans this choral count, Ms. Pierce has several goals in mind. First, she is curious about students' forward counting sequence when the count does not start at 1. Although some of the kindergartners sound fluent in their counting when starting from 1, some of these same students become uncertain when asked to start counting from another number. Ms. Pierce also wonders what students will notice as they reflect on the written record of their count. In the beginning of the year, students' emergent noticings sounded like "I see a 5!" "You wrote the numbers in blue marker," and "The 3 looks like a backward letter *E.*" Ms. Pierce's students have worked hard on the practice of noticing and, as a result of Ms. Pierce's careful facilitating and highlighting of ideas, students are excited about listening to one another's ideas and expanding what they notice.

In addition to mathematical content goals, Ms. Pierce considers goals related to building mathematical community. As she facilitates this choral count, she is mindful of how often students have the opportunity to voice their ideas, how much time she gives them to think and how she helps them to attend to and make sense of one another's ideas. With a couple of months of school under their belts, the kindergartners are building stamina, clarity, and focus in their talk! Suzanne Chapin and colleagues (Chapin, O'Connor, and Anderson 2009) refer to some of these strategies as supporting students to have meaningful discussions.

Ms. Pierce also wants to make sure she uses language that positions all students as capable of constructing important mathematical ideas. She makes sure to show genuine interest in all students' ideas, even, and perhaps especially, emerging ideas and ideas that are incorrect. Ms. Pierce considers how she will encourage wide participation during the choral count and how she might include the voices and ideas of students who are hesitant to share.

"Today, we're going to do a choral count," says Ms. Pierce. "We'll count by 1s, but we're not going to start at 1. We'll start at 5. Think for a moment about what number we will say right after 5."

Students pause to think on their own and then turn and talk to have a chance to say what they think the next few numbers will be. Ms. Pierce notices that while some students immediately know which number comes after 5, some look to the number line or hundred chart in the front of the classroom, while others count from 1 using their fingers. She is happy with this variation because it shows how students draw on many different resources, and picking up a count at any number requires a lot of experience. After students agree that the next number will be 6, they begin the count together. Ms. Pierce uses turn and talks to help each student engage with the task. She records the count on chart paper in front of where the class is seated on the carpet. While some students' voices come in and out of the counting as they go through the teen numbers and over the decades, the momentum of the group keeps the count going. As students say, "42," Ms. Pierce puts her hand out to signal students to stop counting. (See Figure 4.4.)

Ms. Pierce: You stuck with that count all the way to 42! You did it! I heard it get a little tricky with 12, 13, 14, right? Let's try those teens again so we can hear how they sound different. (*Ms. Pierce knows it will take some time for students to feel comfortable with the teens so she gives them all an opportunity to count again with the numbers written out.*) But then when you got to 20,

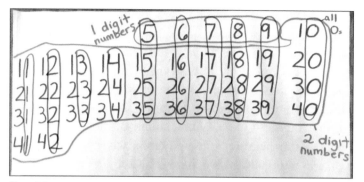

Figure 4.4
Ms. Pierce's class
discusses what they
notice in a count
by 1s.

I heard everyone's voices again. What makes those 20s easier?

Josue: It goes back to 1, 2, 3, 4, 5 again. See, 21, 22, 23, 24, 25.

Ms. Pierce: You're starting to notice some important things. Take a look at our count and the numbers you said! I'm wondering what else you all notice about the numbers in our count. (*Ms. Pierce invites the following children to come up to the chart and show what they see.*)

Matteas: I see the numbers here (*pointing to the first row*) just have one number and the rest of the numbers (*gesturing to the other rows*) have two numbers.

Sophia: The ones on the end (*pointing to the last column*) all have zero. One-zero. Two-zero. Three-zero.

Graciela: Yes, and (*pointing to each column*) these all have 1, and these all have 2, and these all have 3, and these all have 4, all the way down to 9 and then zero.

Cameron: I saw 8, 8, 8 (*pointing to the column with the 8 in the ones place*). Those look like two snakes together.

Ms. Pierce: It sounds like lots of you are noticing that some of these same numbers keep coming up again and again in our counts and in our numbers. Let's look at what Sophia shared. She said the ones on the end all have zero. Let's read these together. (*The children enthusiastically say altogether, "10, 20, 30, 40."*) Do you think we could keep going? What would be next?

Isabel: Five-zero? Six-zero?

Julia: It's still zero, zero!

In September, when Ms. Pierce introduced Choral Counting, much of the focus was on getting the count out, recording it, and hearing a few noticings. Now that students have had some experiences with the Choral Counting routine, Ms. Pierce is excited that many students are starting to notice patterns in the count that will help them start to think about the big ideas of our number system. Students are beginning to notice that some numbers keep popping up in predictable places ("Hey! There's always a 5 going down, down, down that line!") and that change, too, can be predictable ("Look, when you count by 5s it goes zero, 5, zero, 5, zero, 5, forever and ever and ever infinity!") Note that while kindergartners may notice things such as "There are a lot of 2s in this count!"

they may not yet understand *why*. For now the *why* does not need to be the focus of this Choral Counting experience.

Instead, teachers may focus on helping students notice, explain, and elaborate on their noticings and be specific in their language. To support these goals, teachers may ask students questions such as "Can you come up and show me where you see 8, 8, 8? Come and show us!" "Do you see that happening anywhere else here?" or simply "Tell us more about that." They might also be noticing how numbers are written without fully understanding the magnitude of the quantity (three-zero, four-zero). Extending a count down a column or a row, as Ms. Pierce did with 10, 20, 30, 40, can be useful, too, since counting by 1s can support counting by other increments, depending on how the count is written. All of these early noticings will be useful as students learn more about how quantities are composed and decomposed. Ms. Pierce can also invite other students to explain their classmate's pattern: "Can anyone explain what Graciela noticed as she looked across each column?"

As she continues the school year, Ms. Pierce will build on the idea of noticing patterns and building important mathematical ideas in Choral Counting. As she plans her next count, Ms. Pierce decides to build on the idea of "What stays the same?" and "What changes?" She plans to record the count as noted in her plans (see Figure 4.5):

Figure 4.5
Ms. Pierce thinks through what students may notice in a count by 1s starting at 20.

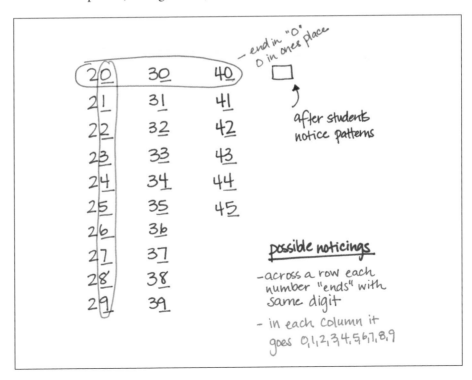

Once again, Ms. Pierce wants to work on counting by 1s from a number other than 1. She also wants to give students a chance to practice and hear the linguistic difference between numbers in the 30s and 40s, which are sometimes merged into one decade by inexperienced counters. However, most important for this count, she plans to continue encouraging the students to make predictions based on the patterns they noticed. After counting to 45 and pausing for noticings, Ms. Pierce plans to draw a box in spot where 50 would go and ask students to predict which number will go in the box. While drawing a box may help students learn how to make a prediction for a certain number, she expects students may want to predict other numbers as well.

Ms. Pierce expects students might have a variety of predictions. She expects some students to say 46, not realizing that the box is not the next number in the count. She expects predictions like one hundred or one million that illustrate that students are guessing that the quantity is greater but not quite sure how to figure out what will be in the box. She also expects that, of the students who predict 50, some will come up with that number by counting on by 1s from 45, while others may use patterns that the class has noticed about that row ("They all end in zero!" "It's counting 2, 3, 4, 5") to make their prediction. Ms. Pierce hopes that asking for predictions in some of her choral counts will send the message that Choral Counting is a sense-making activity and that her students are capable of figuring out important ideas. While drawing a prediction box from time to time may be a helpful practice, it is not a necessary part of every choral count. Just asking students what numbers would appear if you were to continue the count can also offer an open way to discuss predictions and patterns.

Teacher Decisions That Support Student Participation

So what did Mrs. Pierce do in the first month of school to help her student learn how to participate successfully in these counts? Teaching her students how to count together, allowing them to be joyful as they counted the numbers, and inviting them to be curious and share what they notice was foremost in her mind.

Setting Up the Space and Readying Materials

Configuring the space and preparing to record and mark children's noticings are important parts of getting started with choral counts. You will want to think through the features of the space where you will lead the choral count. Many teachers gather students to sit on the floor in their meeting area. They set up chart paper on an easel or use a large whiteboard so that all students can see the record of the count. Having different-colored markers on hand will help you highlight what students are noticing.

Counting with One Voice

Figure 4.6
The recording of the count unfolds as the class counts together joyfully and with one voice.

Depending on the grade level and the count, your voice may help students say the numbers at a common pace. You might expect at first that some students will count too quickly, too slowly, or too energetically. Or you might hear different numbers being said at the same time. Don't be afraid to stop and reset or recount a set of numbers. The written record and voices speaking together lends support. No one person is put on the spot to say the next number. Often teachers will say, "When we count together, we want to make all of our voices sound like one voice. Don't go too fast or too slow. Watch my marker as I'm writing the numbers so you know how fast to go." (See Figure 4.6.) After some repeated practice, saying the numbers as one energized voice becomes a classroom norm.

Sharing Noticings About the Count

A simple invitation, "What do you notice?" opens the door for students to share what they see with one another and with the whole class. Very young children may each want to share something so a well-placed turn and talk at the beginning of the conversation can channel their eagerness to share their ideas. As students gain experience with Choral Counting, they will begin looking for mathematical patterns. Listen closely for mathematical ideas that you may want to highlight or dig into. It's certainly okay if students talk about an interesting feature of the numbers (e.g., some numbers like 22 have the same digit twice or 34 and 43 have digits that are opposite). You do not need to correct or dissuade students from those kinds of noticings; leave open the idea that not everything they share will be a pattern.

Teachers can use many good follow-up questions to help student elaborate on what they see.

"How come it got easier to count when we got here?"

"Come show me where you are seeing that."

"Say more about what you are noticing is changing in the count. What's staying the same?"

"Is that happening anywhere else?"

"What if we keep going? What do you think will happen?"

"What is a number we would say in our count if we kept going?"

"What is a number we would *never* say in our count if we kept going?"

Counting by 10s with First Graders

As young students gain counting and number sense experience, they engage more deeply with the why and the how around their noticings. They begin to develop understandings about place value and our base 10 number system. They consider how numbers relate to one another (e.g., there are ten 10s in 100; you can count to 100 quickly by 5s and 10s, but it takes much longer by 1s).

Many of Mr. Stephens's first graders are fluent in counting by 10s through 100. They happily recite the numbers in a singsong way and have, in previous choral counts, noticed "there's lots of zeros on the end" and "the numbers [referring to the tens place] go up 1, 2, 3, . . ." Mr. Stephens wants to push students' thinking further to a deeper understanding of the base 10 number system, extending the count beyond 100 and connecting the counts to quantity.

One afternoon, Mr. Stephens begins a choral count with his class, counting by 10s, starting at 50. As he anticipated, the first graders have no trouble beginning the count at 50 and then continuing; however, when 100 is reached, many students utter the number with a sense of finality. Surely, the count must be over now!

Mr. Stephens: Could we keep going with our count? Turn and tell your partner what number you think might come next in our count.
(*In planning this pausing point in the choral count, Mr. Stephens anticipated that, along with 110, some students might say 101 or 200, signs they are unsure of how the counting by 10 pattern extends past 100. As he listens to students turn and talk, he hears some of these ideas come up, but he also notices that some pairs of students are silent. Some first graders have not had many opportunities to work with numbers beyond 100.*)

Mr. Stephens: We've heard a few ideas, but many of us aren't sure of what comes next. How could we check?

Elias: We can check on the hundred chart. (*Elias points out a number grid that extends to 120 hanging near the carpet where the students are gathered. Mr.*

Stephens has purposely chosen to display models such as the number grid and number line that extend beyond 100 as tools to support students as they extend their understanding of number beyond 100.)

Mr. Stephens: Elias thinks we should check with the 120 chart. How can we figure out what comes after 100 when we're counting by 10s?

Maya: We can count our numbers. See there's where we started at 40 (*pointing to the 120 chart*). Then 50, 60, 70, 80, 90, and 100. So next is 110. (*Maya touches each number as she points it out to the class and Mr. Stephens underlines the number on the laminated 120 chart with a dry erase marker.*)

Leila: You can also start at 100 (*pointing to that number on the 120 chart*) and just keep counting 10 more.

Mr. Stephens: Let's try what Leila suggested together, ready?

Students in unison: 101, 102, 103, 104, 105, 106, 107, 108, 109, 110.

(*As the class counts, Leila points to 101 through 110 on the number chart while Mr. Stephens puts one finger up for each number counted.*)

Mr. Stephens: So, it looks like we're thinking now that 110 is next. I'll write that down. Let's keep counting. (See Figure 4.7.)

Figure 4.7
Mr. Stephens' recording of counting by 10s starting at 50.

Mr. Stephens asks the students to start back at 80 in order to give them a running start to practice going from 100 to 110. The count continues through 210, with some voices dropping in and out of the count. Mr. Stephens continues with the count despite lots of voices dropping out, but on reaching 210, he asks students to go back to 100 and say the numbers with him again as he points to them in the written count. The record of the count gives students the opportunity to practice the number sequence and keep thinking about the numbers as they read them again.

As Mr. Stephens's class examines the recorded count, they notice patterns. As in past counts, students notice the zero in the ones place. They notice that the tens keep increasing by one. Some students say that the tens "go back to zero," while others see the pattern growing into "ten 10s," "eleven 10s," "twelve 10s," and so on. As students notice the 10s growing, Mr. Stephens marks the jumps of 10 with a different colored marker.

A few comments into the discussion, Nelson notices something that Mr. Stephens wants to pursue.

Nelson: This is like the erasers that me and Emilia counted yesterday.
(*Nelson is referring to a counting collection of pencil-top erasers he and his partner worked on the previous day. Mr. Stephens remembers how excited Nelson and his partner, Emilia, were to count a collection of more than 100 and add a picture of their collection to the "Ways to Count Collections" poster they are making in the classroom. He isn't sure yet, however, what connection Nelson sees between today's count and the counting collection. He's curious though and decides to nudge Nelson to elaborate.*)

Mr. Stephens: That's really interesting that our count is reminding you of your counting collection, Nelson. And it's one we have a picture of right here, right? Can you tell us more about what you're thinking?

Nelson: Like sometimes you can put 10s together to make 100 and then start again with other groups of 10.

Mr. Stephens: Nelson is noticing something important here. Did you all catch that? He's noticing something about groups of 10 in both the count and the collection. Turn and talk to your partner again about what you notice about the connection between how Nelson and Emilia counted the pencil-top erasers and the choral count we just did. (See Figure 4.8.)

As Mr. Stephens kneels next to a few students during the turn and talk, he hears these thoughts:

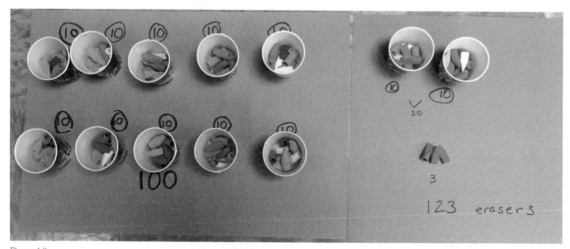

Figure 4.8
Nelson makes a connection between Choral Counting by 10s and the erasers he and Emilia counted by 10s the day before.

Cady: They are both [the Choral Count and the Counting Collection] counting by 10.

Martin: They both have more than 100.

Abdel: 10 groups of 10 is 100 erasers and also 10 groups of 10 is 100 on our counting chart.

In these few minutes, this class of first graders dig into some important big ideas.

- Our number system is based on patterns of 10.
- Patterns in our base 10 number system extend beyond 100.
- Unitizing, which is when a student understands a group of 10 can simultaneously be both 1 group of 10 and 10 groups of 1.
- Connections between patterns in Choral Counting and quantities in Counting Collections.

Considerations for Choral Counting: What to Count by and How Often?

You might be wondering how often to do Choral Counting. It's a routine that students can learn from throughout the year; you will find them looking forward to each opportunity. Depending on how you connect the counts to other aspects of weekly lessons and units, sometimes you might find it useful to do several choral counts in a week. Or you may do a weekly count. There is no right answer.

One important idea about Choral Counting is that it is intentionally designed to be an open-ended activity in which students could work on a range of issues. As you become more familiar with Choral Counting, you may find yourself choosing particular choral counts to support specific curricular topics. Of course, in any unit of instruction, you have particular goals, and with time, you might find that particular counts can be useful when embedded in particular units. Counting by 5-minute increments, starting at 11:00, in a unit on time might be helpful for students to learn what happens when we get to 11:55. If you're exploring even and odd numbers, it would be interesting to count by 2s starting at zero. On another day, it would be interesting to count by 2s starting at 1. Ideas about even and odd can come up in other choral counts as well.

When planning choral counts, you want to keep learning goals for your students in mind. Your grade-level standards may serve as a resource to guide your planning of choral counts. Teachers can also assess students' progress toward big mathematical ideas by closely examining their thinking and strategies as they solve other problems. The standards should not limit the mathematical ideas you explore in your classroom. If your students are ready to move onto larger quantities or bigger counts, explore those ideas in a choral count. The opposite is also true—sometimes older students may revisit a known count in order to uncover new ideas or patterns. For example, third graders may be familiar and fluent in counting by 2s but may revisit this count as they begin to understand ideas around multiplication.

Some counts you plan may respond to specific ideas you see emerging in your classroom. Perhaps you have noticed while Counting Collections by 10s, students are unsure of how to extend this pattern past 100. Is the next group of 10 counted as 101? 200? 110? In this case, Choral Counting by 10s beyond 100 can provide a format for discussing some of these ideas just like in Mr. Stephens's class. Or perhaps you want students to think about the relationship between 5 and 10 so you plan some choral counts by 1s, thinking carefully about how to record the count to bring out ideas of *How many fives in 10? In 20? In 100?* Listening carefully to students' ideas and counting while they are engaged in other instructional activities such as Counting Collections, will provide a lot of information about what choral count sequences can build on the ideas and strategies your students already have.

However, some counts may have less specific mathematical goals. Because Choral Counting is an opportunity for students to reason and to justify, you may choose a count simply because you are curious about the patterns and ideas that will emerge from the discussion. What patterns might students notice if we count by 3s, for example. What strategies will they use to figure out the next number in this count?

Some teachers also pair Choral Counting with other routines like *quick images* or *number talks*. It can be useful to pair Choral Counting with Counting Collections, something we talk more about in the conclusion (see Chapter 8).

More Considerations About How to Record Choral Counts

Earlier, we discussed what you might consider when recording the count. Now that you've seen several examples of Choral Counting in action, let's explore a few more examples of how the recording choices you make allow for different kinds of patterns to emerge and be considered by students. In Ms. Merida's count, the hundreds pattern emerged because of the way she chose to record it.

Counting by 2s

One way of recording this count is in horizontal rows with five numbers in each row to highlight the idea that, when you are counting by 2s, a pattern of 2, 4, 6, 8, and zero repeats in the ones place (see Figure 4.9). While each move to the right on this chart is a jump of 2, each vertical jump between numbers is a jump of 10. This recording also highlights the idea that there are five 2s in each group of 10.

Figure 4.9
Recording of a
count by 2s
horizontally.

2	4	6	8	10
12	14	16	18	20
22	24	26	28	30
32	34	36	38	40
42	44	46	48	50

Some patterns students might notice include the following:

- Going down the column, the digit in the ones place is always the same.
- It goes 10, 20, 30, 40, 50 in the last column.
- The digit in the ones place follows the same pattern in each row: 2, 4, 6, 8, 0.
- It goes up by 10 each row you go down.
- The tens place on the diagonal always goes up by 1, until the end when it goes up by 2.

Another way to record this count is vertically in columns of five, once again to highlight that there are five groups of 2 in each 10. (See Figure 4.10.) This recording the 2, 4, 6, 8, 0 pattern in the ones place as you look down a column.

Figure 4.10
Recording of a
count by 2s
vertically.

2	12	22	32	42
4	14	24	34	44
6	16	26	36	46
8	18	28	38	48
10	20	30	40	50

Here, students might notice:

- The ones place stays the same across each row.
- It goes up by 2 as you go down each row.
- It goes up by 10 as you go across the columns.
- The bottom row is 10, 20, 30, 40, and 50.

Counting by 10s Off Decade

Let's look at four different ways of recording a count by 10s starting at 4. Figures 4.11 and 4.12 highlight that there are ten groups of 10 in each 100.

Figure 4.11
Recording of a count by 10s starting at 4 with ten numbers written horizontally.

4	14	24	34	44	54	64	74	84	94
104	114	124	134	144	154	164	174	184	194
204									

Students might notice:

- All of the numbers have a 4 in the ones place.
- It goes up by 10 across each column.
- It goes up by 100 each row you go down.
- There is 1, 2, 3, 4, 5, 6, 7, 8, 9 in the tens place in the first row.

Figure 4.12
Recording of a count by 10s starting at 4 with ten numbers written vertically.

4	104	204
14	114	
24	124	
34	134	
44	144	
54	154	
64	164	
74	174	
84	184	
94	194	

Here, students might notice:

- All of the numbers have a 4 in the ones place.
- It goes up by 100 across each column.
- It goes up by one 10 as you go down each row.
- It goes 0, 1, 2, 3, 4, 5, 6, 7, 8, 9 when you go down each row.

Figures 4.13 and 4.14 help students see that there are five groups of 10 in each 50, and six groups of 10 in each 60. Students will notice different patterns based on the way the count is recorded. Giving students multiple opportunities to notice patterns and consider ideas is part of the power of the Choral

Counting routine. Look at the patterns students might notice. Try these counts with your students. What else did they notice?

Figure 4.13
Recording of a count by 10s starting at 4 with five numbers written horizontally.

4	14	24	34	44
54	64	74	84	94
104	114	124	134	144

Figure 4.14
Recording of a count by 10s starting at 4 with six numbers written horizontally.

4	14	24	34	44	54
64	74	84	94	104	114
124	134	144	154	164	174

Exploring Backward Counting with Young Learners

Counting forward and backward to 10 is often something young children like to do. Counting backward is more difficult than counting forward and can be particularly challenging for multilingual students as they are building their knowledge of number words in multiple languages. We don't think it's necessary to put a lot of focus on backward counting in the primary grades. As we share an example of a backward choral count, we want to encourage you to be attentive to whether your own students productively engage with backward counting. It might be useful, as a way to test the waters, for example, for you simply to invite students to read a forward choral count, starting at the end. Do your students seem interested? Do they notice something new about the numbers that they didn't when they counted forward?

We do not have clear research evidence that backward counting is strongly connected to children's strategies for subtraction. We know a lot of students use addition to find the difference between two numbers. It is possible, however, that backward counting could support students to use removal strategies in subtraction situations.

Consider, for example, a student thinking about the following problem: *Maria Jose picked 12 flowers from her mother's garden. She gave 5 away to her neighbor next door. How many flowers does she have left?* A young student who has had many experiences with similar take-away problems, as well as a good understanding of counting backward, may think about solving the problem by counting backward and imagining giving away one flower at a time: "11, 10, 9,

8, 7. She has 7 left." A student who cannot as readily count backward might draw 12 circles to represent the flowers, crossing out 5, and counting what is left: "1, 2, 3, 4, 5, 6, 7. She has 7 left." Both strategies will lead to the right answer, and children may be interested in trying out counting backward to solve a problem if that strategy makes sense to them. By second grade, students will encounter subtraction with larger quantities and can use their knowledge of backward counting within our number system in order to find the difference between two numbers. For example, 125 − 37 could be solved by incrementally taking away three 10s and then seven 1s from 125.

Read on to see how a second-grade classroom discussed counting backward by 20, starting at 386.

Counting Backward by 20s in Second Grade

Let's take a look into Ms. Merida's second-grade classroom toward the end of the year, where students are working on counting backward by twenties. Ms. Merida has noticed that many of her students are using their understanding of place value to count backward by 10 when they are solving a subtraction problem. She's curious about what will happen if students try to count backward by 20. How will they keep track? What patterns will they notice? (see Figure 4.15 for her plan.)

Ms. Merida: Today, we're going to do a choral count. We're going to count *backward* by 20s. Let's start at 386. Can you think for a minute to yourself about what two numbers will come next? Please show me a quiet thumb when you think you have an idea of what two numbers comes next.
(*As Ms. Merida watches the students, she notices that some are not sure what numbers will come next. She decides to ask students to do a turn-and-talk in order to give them a chance to check in with each other. After the turn and talk, Ms. Merida calls the students back together. Before starting the count, she asks the students to name the next number and how they figured it out. She intentionally decides to ask this question so that, if any students are not sure how to figure out the next number in the count, they will get to hear a student's strategy for finding the next number. This might support more students to be able to participate in the count.*)

Ms. Merida: Before we start counting, I'm wondering whether anyone can tell me which number comes next and how you figured it out. Markos?

Markos: I think it's 366.

(*Other students use a silent signal to show they have the same answer.*)

Ms. Merida: I see others are agreeing with you. Can you tell us how you got that?

Figure 4.15
Ms. Merida's lesson
plan.

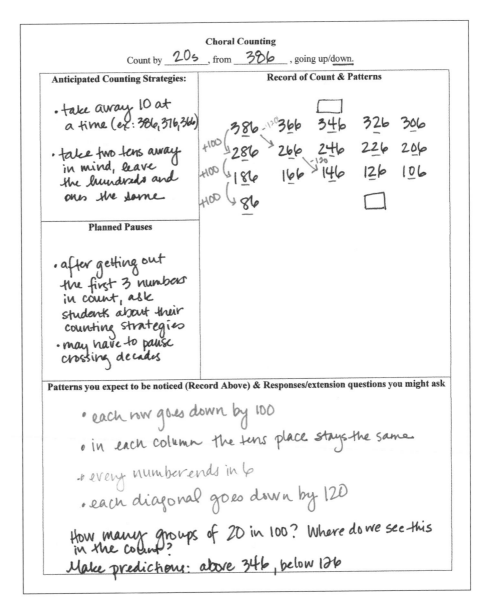

Markos: I subtracted 10 and then subtracted 10 more.

Ms. Merida: Did anyone else do that? You did, Marie? What is 386 – 10?

Marie: It's 376. You just go down 1 from 8.

Ms. Merida: What do you mean you just go down 1 from 8?

Marie: To take 10 away, you just go down 1. 80 then 70.

Ms. Merida: So to take one 10 away from 386, you went from 80 to 70 or you went from eight 10s to seven 10s?

Marie: Umm-hmm.

Ms. Merida: And then what? Markos?

Markos: And then you have to subtract another 10.

Ms. Merida: Okay, so then you go from seven 10s in 376, to six 10s (*writes 366 next to 386*). Can someone use the strategy that Markos and Marie shared with us to find out the number that comes after 366? Kaylea?

Kaylea: It would be 346. You skip the odd numbers.

Ms. Merida: Can you say more about that?

Kaylea: Like I skipped the 5.

Ms. Merida: So if we're counting by 20s, you're saying we are skipping the odd numbers in the tens place? So after 346, what do we skip? (*Some students respond, "336."*)

Ms. Merida: Okay, let's see if that will happen. Let's start back up here (*points to 386*) and keep the count going. (*Students count in unison, saying, "386, 366, 346, 326"; however, when they come to 306, some voices drop out. When they get to the next number in the count, 286, some students start to say, "300." There is some hesitation as students tried to figure out what comes next. Ms. Merida decides to stop to allow students to talk with a partner about what they think the next number is. She could hear many pairs working together to come up with the next number, many believing it was 286.*)

Ms. Merida: What number do we think comes next? (*Students respond, "286."*) Does anyone think it's something different? Okay, if we all agree that it's 286, then I'll write that here. Let's go back to 326, start our count again, and continue from there. (*Students count in unison, saying, "326, 306, 286, 266, 246, 226, 206, 186, 166, 146, 126, 106, 86." Again, some voices drop out around 206 and 186, but there were enough students who identify each number that Ms. Merida decides to keep the count going. There was more hesitancy going from 106 to 86. Students need a few extra seconds to come up with 86. Ms. Merida stop them at 86 so she can ask them to explain the patterns they see. She calls on the first student, Mustafa, to share a pattern he noticed.*)

Mustafa: I see it going down by 1: 3, 2, 1, zero (*points moving his finger down*). (*Ms. Merida underlines the 3 in 386, 2 in 286, 1 in 186, zero as Mustafa points to the numbers.*)

Muna: It's going down by one *hundred*.

Ms. Merida: Muna is helping us see that the number directly below is 100 less. I'm going to record that here (*draws arrows from one column to the next and writes, −100*). What other patterns? (See Figure 4.16.)

Laura: Everything ends in 6.

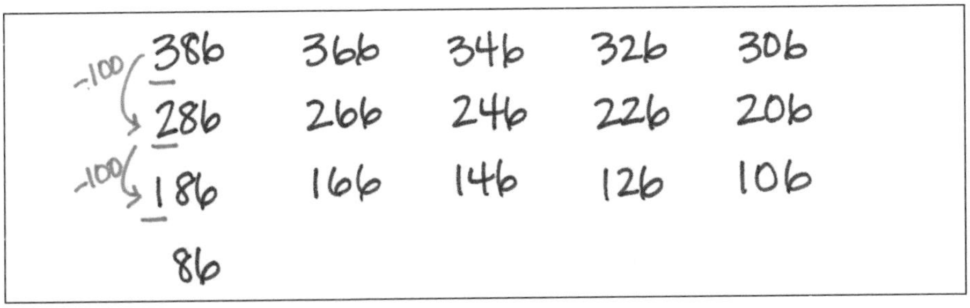

Figure 4.16
Ms. Merida marks what students notice in their backward count.

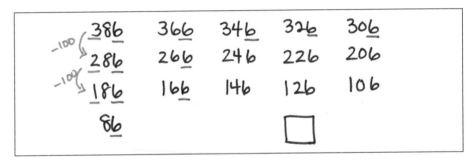

Ms. Merida: Does anyone else see that? (*underlines the 6 across a row and down a column*) Luisa, I see you nodding your head. Do you think this number would end in a 6? (*draws a box under the number 126; Luisa nods yes*) You do? How do you know?

Luisa: Because we're counting by 20s, starting at 386. So, there will always be a 6. (*See Figure 4.17.*)

Figure 4.17
Ms. Merida annotates the backward count as she asks students to predict the number that should come in the recording directly below 126.

Ms. Merida: Who wants to add onto that? Laura, let's come back to you.

Laura: Like Luisa said, we're counting by 20s. So, our ones place won't change. Because only the tens place is changing.

Ms. Merida, (*pointing from 386 to 366*): So the tens place is what is changing here and here. But what about from here to here, what's changing (*pointing from 386 to 286*)?

Laura: Oh, well, the hundreds place is changing. I guess I meant that when we go across the rows, only the tens place is changing.

Ms. Merida, (*pointing from 386 to 286*): Can anyone explain why the hundreds place is changing from here to here?

Samuel: It's because we're counting by 20.

Ms. Merida: Can you say more?

Samuel: We're counting by 20s so it will go up by 100.

Ms. Merida: Does anyone want to add onto that? Maria Jose?

Maria Jose: Because, well, it's like we're counting by groups of 20s. And five 20s is 100.

Ms. Merida: What are people thinking about what Samuel and Maria Jose are saying? Let's see if we can say it in our words and think about if it makes sense.

Gabe: She said that we're counting five groups of 20, which is 100.

Ms. Merida: And how does that help us think about why it goes by 100 when we go down in the column? Does that happen in each column?

Gabe and others: Yes.

Gabe: So, like when we go from 386 to 286, it's like we are counting five times.

Ms. Merida: We are really trying to figure out how to explain what we're seeing. Check in with your neighbor and see if this idea about why the number below every number in our chart is 100 less than the one above it. Is it making sense to you? This won't be the last time we think about this.

In this example (see Figure 4.18), Ms. Merida is using Choral Counting as a warm-up to her main lesson. With time, she thinks some of the backward counting work may help her students in problem-solving situations involving subtraction when they can keep the minuend number whole and jump backward on a number line to subtract the subtrahend amount. For example, $206 - 24$ can be solved by $206 - 10 - 10 - 4$. (See Figure 4.19.)

Figure 4.18
Ms. Merida's class works to connect their observation that five groups of 20 make 100 to their prediction for the number that will go directly below 126.

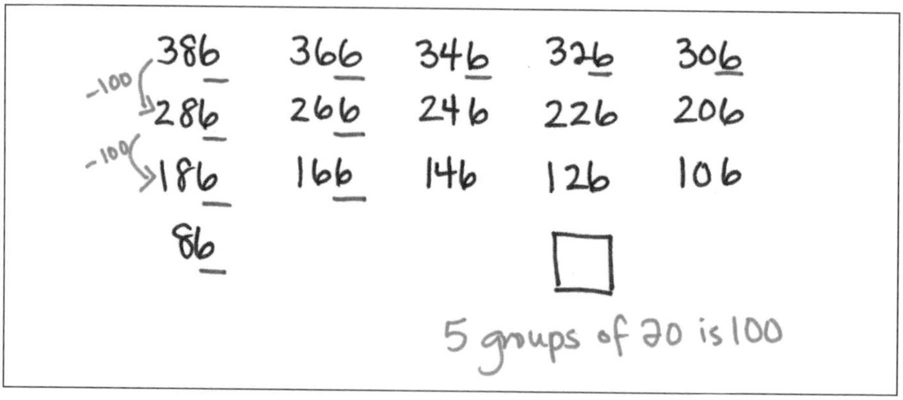

Figure 4.19
The use of the number line to represent one way of solving $206 - 24$ by taking away groups of ten.

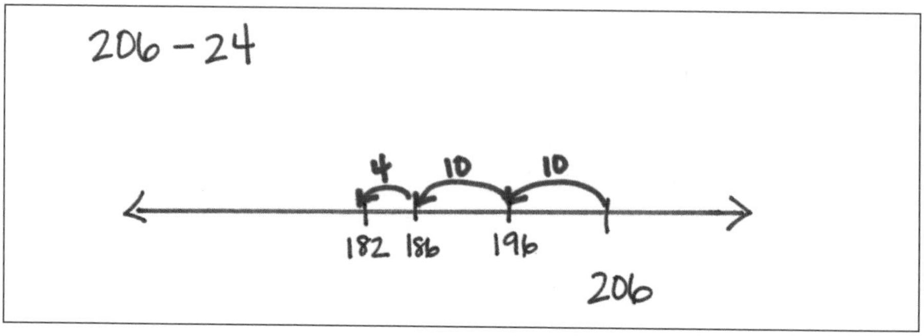

In their work with word problems, she provides further opportunities for students to work on these incrementing strategies through the number choices she selects. For example:

The principal at Parkwood Elementary school wants to give all of the second graders a new notebook that has a picture of their mascot on it, Pete the Panther. There are 206 second graders in all. The principal gave the first classroom 20 notebooks to hand out to their students. How many notebooks does she have left to hand out?

At the beginning of the school year Mr. Brown had 225 pencils for his students to use throughout the school year. By October, Mr. Brown had given out 40 pencils for his students to use. How many pencils does he have left?

The first and second graders at Murphy Elementary School voted on whether they wanted to have cherry or grape popsicles for a treat on their last day of school. After the votes were added up, they found that 166 students wanted cherry and 80 wanted grape. How many more students wanted cherry than grape?

On a busy Saturday, the pizza restaurant made 75 pizzas. On a quieter Monday, they only made 45 pizzas. How many more pizzas did they make on Saturday night than on Monday night?

Extending Choral Counting in First Grade

Later in the school year, Mr. Stephens's students have become stronger at not only noticing patterns but also hypothesizing *why* these patterns occur. They also make connections between counts, comparing and contrasting patterns and why two counts might be similar or different. Students have also spent significant time learning how to talk to one another about their mathematical ideas. The conversation flow is less back and forth between teacher-student-teacher-student and more of a conversation among students with the teacher facilitating and guiding students to dig in deeper around important ideas.

Mr. Stephens's first-grade class has spent much of the year investigating patterns in the base 10 number system. The class has regularly choral counted by 10s starting on decades or in-between decades and has noticed many patterns underlying the base 10 number system. However, Mr. Stephens has noticed that while many students can say, "The ones stay the same" or "It's 7, 7, 7, 7, 7 in all the numbers," he is not yet convinced that students know *why* this pattern is happening. Mr. Stephens plans to support his students to understand *why* by bringing in quantity. He plans to connect a choral count by building a model of the count using sticks of ten Unifix cubes and loose cubes, a material and model with which students are familiar.

For most choral counts, Mr. Stephens's class sits in a group facing the chart paper where the count will be recorded. Today, however, Mr. Stephens asks students to sit in a circle so they can still see the chart paper but can also see the Unifix cubes in the middle of the circle.

Mr. Stephens: We've really thought a lot about counting by 10s in first grade. Today, we're going to do another count by 10s, but we're going to make something as we count. Look at what I have here in the middle of the circle. (*Mr. Stephens has placed two sticks of ten Unifix cubes each and 6 loose cubes in the center of the circle. A tray of sticks of ten and loose Unifix cubes is also on a tray in the center of the circle.*)

Cady: I see 26.

Mr. Stephens: Did anyone else see that? Gabe, why did Cady say 26?

Gabe: She counted 10, 20 and then that's 6, so 26.

Abdel: Or she counted 10, 20, 21, 22, 23, 24, 25, 26.
(*Most students are nodding or showing the connection hand signal that the class uses as a silent "I agree," or "I'm thinking that, too" sign, so Mr. Stephens keeps going.*)

Mr. Stephens: Today, as we count by 10, starting at 26, I'm going to ask Elias to add cubes each time to show the number we say. So, what might Elias be doing with the Unifix cubes?

Elias: I'm going to add a ten stick.

Alejandra: He might get enough to make 100.

Mr. Stephens: Well, let's try it out. Your job, like always, is to say the numbers as we count at a medium speed. Your eyes can be watching my marker as we record the numbers, but you can also be watching what Elias is doing with the Unifix cubes. Then we'll stop and notice some things about the numbers we wrote and see what's happening with the cubes.

Mr. Stephens has chosen Elias to help build the quantity because he has noticed that Unifix cubes organized in ten sticks and loose cubes are a tool and model with which Elias feels comfortable. He is hoping that this building role in the count will give Elias and his class an opportunity to investigate the connections between a familiar model and the patterns recorded in the count. As the students count, Elias adds a ten stick to the original pile of 26. Mr. Stephens stops the count at 246.

Mr. Stephens: Okay, so you were busy during this count! Your voices were counting; your eyes were watching the numbers I wrote *and* what Elias was doing with the cubes. And your brain was thinking, noticing, and pattern-finding. Let's turn and talk to your partner about what you noticed in this count.

(*After the students talk to their partner, Mr. Stephens calls on some of them to share their ideas.*)

Maya: My partner, Leila, and I saw the same thing. The 6 stays the same.

Nelson: That's called the ones.

Mr. Stephens, *underlines the 6 in each number with a green marker.* That's interesting. That 6 digit never changed. We have noticed that in the past when we've counted by 10s. The ones don't change. (*Mr. Stephens points to two recent choral count recordings of counting by 10 from various numbers in which the students noticed this same pattern.*) So, where could we see that pattern in what Elias was doing with the Unifix cubes?

Chantel: It's the 6 loose cubes.

Leila: Those six 1s are never changing. Elias just kept adding a ten stick, ten stick, ten stick. He never touched the 1s. He never took new loose cubes from the tray.

Mr. Stephens: I noticed that, too. So, let's talk with our partners again. We noticed there's a 6 in the ones place in *all* of our numbers. We noticed Elias never touched the six 1s in the middle of our circle. But, *why?* Why is that happening in *this count?* Go ahead and turn and talk.

During the turn and talk, Mr. Stephens circulates through several groups listening and jotting quick notes on his clipboard. Some main ideas come up in the conversations.

- Only the tens change. The tens place goes 2, 3, 4, 5, 6, 7, 8, 9, 10, 11, 12 . . .
- The tens and the hundreds change. Then tens place goes 2, 3, 4, 5, 6, 7, 8, 9, then 0 in the tens place because there's 100.
- The 6 cubes stay the same because you're never adding any 1s. (This is a response we hear students say. Our work as teachers is to help them express that they are adding ten 1s each time, which results in an increase of the numeral in the tens place.)

Using the Unifix cube model has clarified some ideas for these students around place value, but it's also brought up some interesting ideas around groups of 10s and 100s. Mr. Stephens knows that true and deep understanding of place value is complex and takes time. His noticings of students' talk and the ideas that emerge from this choral count will help him plan future choral counts, as well as inform his daily math work to continue to offer opportunities for students to fully construct place value understanding.

We share this vignette not because we think Choral Counting has to involve the use of physical materials, but because we want to give you an image of how teachers can adapt a familiar activity structure as well as try something new to see whether it's helpful for students. That's an important idea. There aren't right and wrong ways to lead these instructional activities. You should feel free to experiment and generate new ideas. For example, one teacher experimented with an old choral count by covering up certain numbers with sticky notes to see whether the patterns students noticed would help them figure out what numbers were covered.

Conclusion

Counting is a common activity in primary classrooms. Through Choral Counting, young children have opportunities to learn important aspects of counting and about our place value system. Choral counts can help young children to learn the sequence as they count aloud together, first by ones and later by other increments. Further, children have opportunities to reason, to predict, and to justify as they look for patterns and notice what happens to numbers as they count together. We believe that Choral Counting can help primary teachers with an important goal they have for their students, to develop identities as mathematical thinkers.

* * *

Choral Count Examples to Get You Started

As you become more experienced with Choral Counting, you will notice student thinking that will help guide your thinking as you plan the next choral count. However, it's always helpful to have possible ideas when you are not sure of the next step. The chart that follows suggests counts for these times. We have grouped the counts by big mathematical ideas that you may want to work on with your students. It is our hope that you will examine these suggestions and consider which might be useful in your classroom as you work toward designing choral counts that support your community of mathematicians.

Planning choral counts collaboratively with colleagues is one of the best ways to investigate the practice of Choral Counting. Consider planning a series of choral counts at team meetings or reach out to the larger community of math teachers on social media who are also thinking about Choral Counting by tweeting a question or a thought with the hashtag #choralcounting. Visit tedd.org to learn more about Choral Counting and view videos on Choral Counting in action in primary and upper grades classrooms. (See Appendix 3 for more links to websites, videos, and blog posts to support your use of Choral Counting.)

Choral Counting Examples to Try in the Primary Grades		
Counts	**Mathematical Ideas**	**Examples**
Counts by 1s		
By 1s, starting from 1	• Patterns in the base 10 number system • Fluency counting by 1s, especially in teen numbers and across decades	1 to 50
By 1s, starting from a number other than 1	• Patterns in the base 10 number system exist, regardless of the starting point of the count • Fluency counting on from numbers other than 1	12 to 60 18 to 58 39 to 99 See "Counting by 1s with Kindergartners" (p. 84)
By 1s, backward	• Comparing patterns found when counting forward to when counting backward • Fluency counting backward by 1s	10 to 0 30 to 0 28 to 8 86 to 50 *(continued)*

By 1s, going beyond 100	• Patterns in the number system beyond 100 • Fluency counting by 1s over 100	80 to 120 see "Choral Counting and the Community of Mathematicians" (p. 77)
By 1s, with three- and four-digit numbers	• Patterns in the number system within three-digit numbers • Place value • Fluency counting with three-digit numbers and crossing over 1,000	175 to 205 387 to 421 985 to 1,020

Counts by 10s, 5s, and 2s

| By 10s on decade
By 10s off decade
By dimes | • Patterns in the base 10 number system
• There are ten 10s in each hundred
• Fluency with counting by 10s, making jumps of 10
• Connection to computation strategies
• Connection to dimes | By 10s, starting at 26
 |

| By 5s
By nickels | • Patterns when skip-counting by 5s
• Connection between counting by 5s and counting by 10s
• There are two 5s in each 10
• There are twenty 5s in each 100
• Connection to nickels and dimes
• Fluency counting by 5s | By 5s, from 75 to 300
 |
| By 2s | • Patterns when skip-counting by 2s
• There are five 2s in each 10
• Even and odd numbers
• Fluency counting by 2s | |

(continued)

Counts by 20s and 100s		
By 100s	• Patterns in the base 10 number system • Place value • There are ten 100s in each thousand • Fluency making jumps of 100 • Connection to strategies for addition	Backward by 20s, starting at 386 -100 ⌠ 386 366 346 326 306 　　⌡ 286 266 246 226 206 -100 ⌠ 186 166 146 126 106 　　　 86 　　　　　　　5 groups of 20 is 100 • every number ends in 6 • each row goes down by 100
By 100s	• Patterns in the base 10 number system • Place value • There are ten 100s in each thousand • Fluency making jumps of 100 • Connection to computation strategies	By 100, starting at 104 +500 ⌠ 104 204 304 404 504 +500 ⌠ 604 704 804 904 1004 +500 ⌠ 1104 1204 1304 1404 1504 +500 ⌠ 1604 1704 1804 1904 2004 +500 ⌠ 2104 • down each column goes the same pattern in tens place 1,6,1,6,1 2,7,2,7 3,8,3,8 　the digits alternate between 2 numbers 5 apart • each number ends in 4 • every row you go down, it goes up by 500 • there is always a zero in the tens place • if you look @ the hundreds place, it goes up 1,2,3,4.... 17,18,19,20 01 • the numbers increase by 600 on diagonal

Count by other numbers		
By 25s	• There are four 25s in 100 • Connection to quarters and dollars • Place value • Composing and decomposing numbers • Supports computation strategies that involve decomposing numbers	By 11s, starting at 11 By 12s, 12 to 240 By 15s, 15 to 300 11 22 33 44 55 } +50 +5 66 77 88 99 110 } +50 +5 121 132 143 154 165 176 187 198 209 • in the ones place, it goes 1,6,1,6 2,7,2,7 • before the number is 3 digits, the tens place + ones place is the same number • it goes up by 5 tens + 5 ones in the last column

Reference

Chapin, Suzanne, Catherine O'Connor, and Nancy Canavan Anderson. 2009. *Classroom Discussions: Using Math Talk to Help Students Learn, Grades K–6*. Sausalito, CA: Math Solutions.

CHAPTER 5

Choral Counting 3–5

by Teresa Lind and Kendra Lomax

Ms. Li's fourth-grade class is gathered at the carpet, analyzing a choral count by 4s that they have just counted together. "If we kept counting, do you think would we land on 326?" Ms. Li asks. "Is 326 a multiple of 4?" (See Figure 5.1.)

Ms. Li's class is engaged in a counting activity. While counting has often been seen as a primary student's task, there is still plenty of counting work to be done in the upper grades. In Ms. Li's class, Choral Counting provides an opportunity for students to explore the relationship between factors and multiples.

Figure 5.1
Ms. Li's class considers whether they will land on 326 if they keep counting by 4.

We'll hear more from her students later in this chapter. Consider the strategies you use in your daily life to mentally compute when you're splitting a check at a restaurant or adding up your bills. Many of the strategies that children (and adults) use in adding, subtracting, multiplying, and dividing demand knowledge of the number system well beyond 100 or even 1,000. Knowing which number comes before 1,200, what is 100 more than 4,951, how many 12s there are in 24,000, or how close 7,690 is to another thousand are examples of the kind of number knowledge we draw on daily to compute and estimate. Older students also consider numbers in between whole numbers: fractions and decimals. Just as young children need lots of experiences to learn about whole numbers, so, too, must older students have many experiences counting by fractional and decimal amounts to gain familiarity with their relative sizes and positions within our counting system.

Children's mathematical ideas are central to Choral Counting. The introduction to this book provides an overview of Choral Counting (see Chapter 1). In this activity, the teacher leads students in counting aloud together by a given number. As they count, the teacher carefully records the count for all to see and then facilitates a discussion about the patterns students notice within the count. Chapter 4 describes Choral Counting in the primary grades, and in this chapter, we consider the continued opportunities Choral Counting holds for students in third through fifth grades. This instructional activity is a chance for students and teachers to play with number, operation, and patterns. Every student can contribute by calling out the count in unison. There are endless patterns for students to notice, to discuss, and to extend. Students can engage in reasoning about, predicting, and justifying why particular patterns occur. Teachers can keep the conversation broad and exploratory or encourage children to consider particular mathematical ideas through their selection of tasks and their facilitation of the conversation. Choral Counting in the upper grades lends itself well to exploring a variety of mathematical ideas, including

- developing skip-counting skills that support students' multiplication and division strategies
- exploring the meaning and relative size of fractions and decimals
- extending ideas about the operations with whole numbers to operating with fractions and decimals
- gaining experience with units of measurement and converting between units
- leveraging counting ideas in problem-solving situations
- engaging in mathematical practices, such as looking for and making use of structure and constructing and critiquing arguments about patterns within the count

We will explore here how these big mathematical ideas can be worked on through Choral Counting.

Choral Counting with Whole Numbers: Exploring Place Value

What patterns do you notice within this choral count? (Figure 5.2).

Figure 5.2
Counting by 200s
starting at 5,000.

5000	6000	7000	8000
5200	6200	7200	8200
5400	6400	7400	
5600	6600	7600	
5800	6800	7800	

Maybe you noticed or predicted:

- All of the numbers are even numbers and end in zero.
- Each column begins with the same digit: there's the 5,000 column, 6,000, 7,000, 8,000.
- The hundreds place stays the same in each row. In the second row, each number has a 2 in the hundreds place.
- If you look diagonally, starting from 5,000 and going right, the number increases by 1,200. This is true starting with any number.
- The number straight across from 7,800 will be 8,800.
- The next number in the counting sequence after 8,200 would have 4 in the hundreds place.
- In the next column, every number would start with 9,000.

Can you put into words *why* those patterns occur? What mathematical ideas could children discuss through this count? Choral counts like this one can provide important opportunities for students to extend their early ideas about the counting sequence to develop generalizations about the structure of the base 10 number system for increasingly larger quantities.

To get a better picture of what it might look like to work on place value ideas through Choral Counting, let's step inside Ms. Coleman's third-grade class. On this September morning, the students will try the same count: counting by 200 starting from 5,000. Ms. Coleman has selected this count in order to surface some big ideas about place value. In earlier lessons, students have expressed that they know how many 100s there are in a given number by looking at the hundreds place. This begs the question: 5,000 has a zero in the hundreds place, but does that mean there are zero hundreds contained in the number? Or, can we see 5,000 in other ways, like fifty 100s or 1,000 and forty 100s? Ms. Coleman knows her students will need more robust ways of composing and decomposing number in order to operate with large numbers. Through this count, she hopes to begin broadening the conversation about the composition of numbers. Instead of counting by 100, this time she selects 200 so that students can consider a new question: How many 200s must you count to make 1,000? She anticipates that the students won't have too much trouble counting, but that it may be a challenge to express the idea that 5 groups of 200 make a new thousand.

Ms. Coleman: Today, we're going to do another choral count. Remember, when we count it's important to watch my pen so that we can say each number together. Today, we will count by 200. We aren't going to be starting from zero though; we're going to start counting from 5,000! Think about what the first few numbers will be and show me a silent thumb at your chest when you're ready to begin.

This is one of their first choral counts together, although many students have experienced Choral Counting in the primary grades. Ms. Coleman reminds students of their norms for participating before they begin. Gathered on the carpet together, the students begin counting from 5,000. When they reach 6,600, Ms. Coleman asks students to pause.

Ms. Coleman: This sounds pretty smooth! We've never counted by 200. How are you figuring out what number comes next?
(*Students share a few ways they are calculating the next number. Some students are counting the hundreds by 2s: 52, 54, 56. Others notice the pattern of the hundreds increasing by 2.*)

Pausing early in the count to elicit different computation strategies allows students to hear a range of strategies for determining the next number, supporting all students to engage in the counting.

The students begin counting again, this time starting at 6,000 to get a running start. When the students reach 8,200, Ms. Coleman stops them once more. This time she asks students to look for patterns.

Ms. Coleman: What do you notice about these numbers? Think to yourself.
(*After allowing students to discuss what they notice in pairs, she brings the class back together.*)

Faiza: The same pattern happens in each column: 2, 4, 6, 8.

Ms. Coleman: You see it goes 2, 4, 6, 8 in the hundreds place. (*She underlines the repeating digits for the rest of the class. See Figure 5.3.*) Did anyone else see that pattern?
(*Students use a silent signal to show they agree or had a similar idea. Ms. Coleman invites Sahra to share what she was telling her partner, knowing that the conversation she was having with her partner during turn and talk might help the class move toward her mathematical goal.*)

Figure 5.3
Ms. Coleman's annotations as students share patterns they notice.

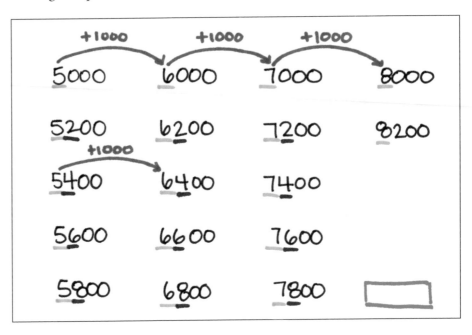

Sahra: I told Hector, I see 5-5-5-5-5, 6-6-6. (*Sahra points to the thousands place in each column.*)

Hector: And for 7 and 8, too. It's adding 1,000 to each column.

Ms. Coleman: Does that only happen here, with 5,000, 6,000, 7,000?

Hector: No, it happens all over. Like 5,400 to 6,400.

Ms. Coleman: I have another question. What do you think will go here? (*She places a box farther down in the count where 8,800 would go.*) Turn and talk with your neighbor. What number will go in the box, and how do you know?

In this exchange, Ms. Coleman asks for clarification about where Sahra and Hector's pattern occurs. She then invites the whole class to use the patterns that have been shared so far by asking what number will go in the box. Asking students to turn and talk allows Ms. Coleman to listen to pairs of students to hear how they're reasoning about the missing number. After a brief turn-and-talk, Ms. Coleman calls them back together.

Beth: You can see that it's next to 7,800. I knew if you go to the other side, to the 8,000s, it would be 8,800.

Kristine: I agree with Beth. She started at 5,800, then she added 1,000 and got to 6,800. Then she added 1,000 more and got to 7,800. So 1,000 more would be 8,800.
(*As Kristine explains, Ms. Coleman points to the numbers and notates the jumps of 1,000 between columns for all students to see.*)

Ms. Coleman: I wonder why that is happening.
(*After a long pause, she asks students to discuss with their partner why the pattern of adding 1,000 from one column to the next is happening.*)

Omar: Well, Paula said . . . (*Omar hesitates*).

Paula: I said that we're going by 200, so it takes us 5 times to get to 6,000.

Michael: What I said to my partner is that 5,000 plus 200 is 5,200 and 5,200 plus 200 is 5,400. And I know that because 2 plus 2 is 4.

Ms. Coleman: Okay, so you are helping us think about how to add the 200s, Michael. I want to come back to what Paula and Omar said. They were thinking that it takes five 200s to make 1,000. What do we think about that?

Jordan: I agree with them. You take five 200s to get to the next thousand.

Ms. Coleman: If you look at our columns, did you notice that there are five numbers? What's going on between 5,000 and 6,000?
(*With this question, she begins pressing students to begin to explain the connection between 1,000 in each column and five 200s.*)

Thomas: You're adding 1,000 like from 5,800 to 6,800 and 6,800 to 7,800. It's the same as the top. It's 5,000 to 6,000 and 7,000 and 8,000.

Carrie: Yeah, because five 200s is 1,000. It doesn't matter where you start.

Ms. Coleman: Okay, let's count by 200. We said it took five 200s to get to the next thousand. Let's count 5 groups of 200 and see what we land on.
(*The students count: 5,000, 5,200, 5,400, 5,600, 5,800, 6,000.*)

Ms. Coleman: Did it work? (*Students nod in agreement.*) Think about what you just did. If we kept counting, would we land on 10,000? How do you know?

Sahra: I think 10,000 is a million maybe? It goes like . . . 2 times 5 equals 10, so two 5,000s would be 10,000.

Omar: We're counting by 200s and 200s always get us to the next thousand. Five 200s is 1,000. So, if we're on 9,800 another 200 will get us to the next thousand. And if we keep counting by 200, that's how we're going to get to the next thousand.

Omar adds onto Sahra's second idea that 2 times 5 is 10, so 2 groups of 5,000 would be 10,000. This important mathematical contribution allowed the class to continue grappling with the relationships between 200, 1,000, and 10,000. But you might be confused by Sahra's initial statement, "I think 10,000 is a million maybe." Ms. Coleman wasn't quite sure what to think about this statement in the moment either. Later in the day, Ms. Coleman talked with Sahra about her "million" idea. Through their discussion, Ms. Coleman discovered that Sahra was trying to reason about the number of 200s it would take to get to 10,000. She knew there must be *many* 200s in 10,000 and expressed this idea with one of the biggest numbers she knows about: a million! Sahra was reasoning about the size of 10,000. It is sometimes a challenge to follow the logic of a child's idea in the midst of a choral count, but don't be too quick to dismiss ideas that at first seem confusing or incorrect. Instead, get curious about the thinking behind these ideas. There are likely to be moments in a choral count when you're not sure how to respond to a student's idea or whether it will move your discussion toward productive mathematics. In these moments, you could pluck out a piece of the idea like Omar did, ask a student to try to repeat the idea, or tell the student honestly, "I need more time to think about this. Can I ask you more about it later today?" Teachers are learners, too!

Getting Started with Choral Counting

How did Ms. Coleman get her class to have these kinds of mathematical discussions in September? Don't worry if your students are just beginning to develop norms for discussion. You may find that Choral Counting serves as an excellent routine through which students can learn how to explain their thinking and how to productively agree, disagree, or add onto one another's ideas.

When you first begin Choral Counting with your students, you will need to introduce the activity and help students know how to participate: "First we will count together and then we'll look at our count and notice patterns." It's helpful to set clear expectations for *how* to count together. Let students know what their volume and pacing should sound like with directions: "When we count, we want to stay together. Watch as I write each number to know when to say the next one. Also, we want to be able to hear one another. Try to count so that you are louder than a tiny whisper but not so loud that the classroom next door will hear us."

Also consider where students will sit. We recommend gathering students on the carpet around a whiteboard or an easel, rather than having students seated at desks. A unified choral voice is an important and intentional feature of the activity. When students are spread out, their voices are more isolated and distinct than when they are seated together. There will be moments when some students *don't* know the next number to say. This is expected and perfectly okay. The choral voice will carry on, allowing students to rejoin the counting. Also, having students on the carpet makes it easy for students to see the count, for students to turn and talk to one another, and for you to see and hear the students.

Forward and Backword Counts to Support Students' Understanding of Place Value

Your selection of Choral Counting tasks will depend on the particular mathematical and social goals you have in mind. One exciting feature of Choral Counting is the flexibility to have a very open-ended discussion about patterns in our number system or to design a count to work toward a specific mathematical goal. We encourage you to try both of these approaches. Consider what mathematical ideas you want students to explore and what you hope to learn about your students' thinking. Pay attention to students' counting during other activities and get curious about their computational errors. These can be great sources for future choral counts! Counting backward is more challenging than counting forward, perhaps because children have much more experience counting forward. The ability to count backward may be particularly useful for mentally subtracting and dividing, so we recommend including these in your counting repertoire.

Figure 5.4 shows Ms. Coleman's plan for a backward choral count later in the year. (You can find blank planning sheets in Appendix 2.) She intentionally selected this count backward by 10 to support students' work in subtraction, hoping to make some connections to strategies like counting back by 10s and 100s. After they completed the count, she put the chart up on the wall for students to refer to later. In her planning, notice how she has selected strategic moments to pause and let students think about what the next number will be (see Figure 5.4). Ms. Coleman also anticipated patterns that students might notice, allowing her to consider in advance how to represent these patterns.

One thing to note about backward choral counts is that, depending on the number you begin with, you may open up conversations about numbers less

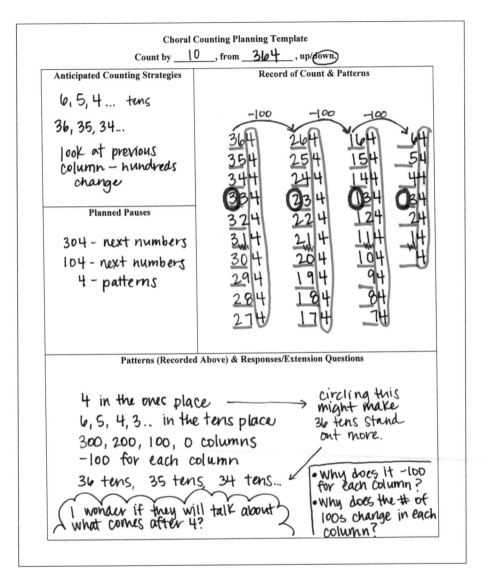

Figure 5.4
Ms. Coleman's plan for a backwards count by 10 starting at 364.

than zero. For example, in Ms. Coleman's backward count by 10, the students might wonder what comes after 4. Does it just stop? This is an excellent question! You might acknowledge that there are numbers less than zero and continue pursuing your other mathematical goals for the conversation, or you could have a more extended conversation about what "less than zero" means. Be prepared to meet these questions with some wonder and curiosity. You don't have to neatly resolve the meaning of negative numbers in the upper grades, but these early conversations set students up well to encounter negative numbers in their future mathematical careers.

Here are some other examples of counts that might encourage students to consider place value ideas. (See the end of the chapter for more sample counts.)

- Count forward by 10 or 100 starting from 2,800 to engage students in discussions about how many 10s or 100s fit inside a given number.
- Count by 20 backward from 700 or 710 to build counting skills that might support subtraction strategies.
- Count forward or backward by 10 from 6,865 to develop familiarity and flexibility counting with larger numbers.
- Count forward by 90, which can also be thought of as counting forward 100 and back 10.
- Count forward or backward by multiples of 10 to make connections between multiplying by other factors, for example, counting by 2 and 20 or 3 and 30.

Choral Counting to Develop Ideas About Multiplication and Division

Choral Counting can also be used to support other mathematical goals in the upper grades, such as helping students develop their understanding of multiplication and division. Multiplication and division rely on making use of equal-size groups, and counting repeatedly by the same number matches the structure of these operations. A teacher may plan a choral count by single-digit numbers to create an opportunity for students to think about patterns that surface through the repeated addition of these equal-size groups and explore why the patterns exist.

Exploring Multiplication: Counting by Multiples of 4

Let's revisit Ms. Li's Choral Count from the beginning of the chapter. Ms. Li has planned this count by 4s, building on the work her students have been doing with factors and multiples. Ms. Li's goal is for her fourth graders to use the patterns they notice within the count to make predictions about which numbers will or will not be a multiple of 4.

Ms. Li explains that today they will choral count by 4 and asks the students to think of the first three numbers. When the students quietly show a thumbs-up at their chest, she knows the class is ready to begin. The class starts counting, "4, 8, 12 . . ." (See Figure 5.5.) After a few numbers, they stop to share how they know the next number and then continue counting until they reach 60. Ms. Li asks them to share the patterns they see that helped them count.

Amy: It goes 4-4-4, 8-8-8.

Ms. Li: Where do you see the 4s?

Amy: In the first column. In the ones place.

> (*Ms. Li puts a box around the 4s in the first column. She asks Amy to tell her where she sees the 8s and marks these digits, too. She asks Amy these questions in order to encourage the class to use increasingly precise language to describe the patterns they see.*)

Keiko: Each row goes up by 20. 20 plus 20 is 40. 16 plus 20 is 36. So all you have to do is add 20 more.

Ms. Li: That's an interesting pattern. Why do you think each row increases by 20?

Kyle: I think it's because if you count by 4 five times you get 20.

> (*Ms. Li asks for someone to revoice Kyle's idea, and they count the five 4s together. She asks students to make a prediction about what will go below 48. See Figure 5.6.*)

Ms. Li: Could you use the patterns in the count to help you predict what number would go here?

> (*After students have had time to talk with their partners, Ms. Li asks them to share their ideas.*)

Kaleb: I think it's 68. *Many students show that they agree using a silent signal.* I know because the 8 stays the same, and I added 2 more.

Nakia: I agree that it's 68 and that the 6 stays the same. But I added 20 more. I think Kyle meant 2 more 10s.

> (*Ms. Li has the class continue counting to see whether they are correct. She draws another*

Figure 5.5
Ms. Li records the count as children count by 4s.

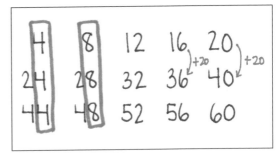

Figure 5.6
Ms. Li's class considers why the numbers are increasing by 20 as you read down a column.

box two spaces below 52, asking again for a prediction. Because the class was able to predict these numbers with ease, she decided to ask the students a question that would prompt them to use the patterns they've seen and to begin to make conjectures about multiplying by 4.)

Ms. Li: If we kept counting, do you think would we land on 326? Is 326 a multiple of 4? Why or why not?

(Ms. Li provides individual time to think and then asks students to talk with their partners. As students talk, Ms. Li listens to see how students use the patterns that they've identified to predict whether or not a number might be a multiple of 4.)

Lisa: Maybe. It's an even number like all of the other count-by-4 numbers.

James: And it ends in 6 like 16, 36, 56, 76.

Ms. Li: Lisa and Mario say 326 might be a multiple of 4. How could we use the patterns that we've noticed to help us know for sure?

Mario: I don't think it's a multiple of 4. Because they're all odd in the tens place in that column. Like 1, 3, 5. It's not even in the tens place like 126.

(Ms. Li asks two people to revoice Mario's idea to highlight this important noticing. Then she asks if 326 could appear in another column.)

Kylie: It couldn't appear in the first column because in each column the tens goes up by 2 tens. Like the first column is zero tens, 2 tens, 4 tens, 6 tens, and if you kept going it would be 8 tens, 10 tens. But they all end with 4: 44, 64, 84. Not a 6.

(Ms. Li wraps up the choral count by asking students to describe the strategies they might use to determine whether a number is a multiple of 4.)

Relating Multiple Counts: "Are Multiples of 8 Also Multiples of 4 and Multiples of 2? Why?"

Teachers may find it useful to ask students to make connections between two or more choral counts in order to think about how multiples of given numbers are related. In the following vignette, Ms. Brown's fourth-grade class explores factors and multiples using a set of choral counts from the previous few days. The class has already counted by 2 and 4, relatively easy choral counts that they had already done in previous grades as they explored skip-counting. Today, Ms. Brown has planned for the students to count by 8 and examine patterns among the three related counts, thinking about which numbers show up on all three counts and why. Look at the counts (Figure 5.7): What do you notice?

Maybe you noticed:

2	4	6	8	10
12	14	16	18	20
22	24	26	28	30
32	34	36	38	40

4	8	12	16	20
24	28	32	36	40
44	48	52	56	60
64	68	72	76	80

8	16	24	32	40
48	56	64	72	80
88	96	104	112	120
128	136	144	152	160

Figure 5.7
Counting by 2, 4, and 8. What do you notice?

- Every number is an even number.
- The numbers in the count by 2 double when you look at the count by 4. They double again in the count by 8.
- In every column, the ones place stays the same.
- The numbers in the final column in each count is a multiple of 10.
- Looking at the rows, the tens place doesn't follow a consistent pattern from one count to another. In the count by 2, the tens place is zero for five numbers, then 1 for five numbers, and continues on. For the count by 4, the tens place is zero for two numbers, 1 for two numbers, but 2 for three numbers. And in the count by 8, the tens place goes 0, 1, 2, 3, 4, 4, 5, 6, 7, 8.
- The ones place in each row follows the same counting by 2, 4, or 8 pattern. Also, starting with the first number in each count, if you look diagonally, the ones place follows the same counting by 2, 4, or 8 pattern.

Ms. Brown planned out all three counts together because she knew she wanted to make it easy for students to make connections across them. She began by writing out the counts both vertically and horizontally, with different amounts of numbers in the rows and columns, to see what patterns emerged. We invite you to play around with how you might write out the count, too (see our online planning tool sten.pub/choralcounting). While you could write out a count that has complicated or obscure patterns, it is ideal to plan a count that has interesting patterns that are readily visible. This will encourage broad participation and allow you to focus on structure within the number system. Ms. Brown looked at the various options for recording the count and decided to write the numbers horizontally with five numbers in each row because it highlights the repetition in the ones place and has a nice stopping point at the twentieth multiple. She used the same structure for all three counts to help students to notice the similarities between them.

Anticipating her students' thinking, and how she will make these ideas visible, allowed Ms. Brown to plan questions to press the students to think about the connections between their three counts using questions such as, "What do these three counts have in common? Are multiples of 8 also multiples of 4 and multiples of 2? Why?"

Ms. Brown: Today, we're going to do a tricky choral count. We're going to count by 8! How can you use these counts from the past two days (*pointing to the two previous choral counts*) to help you count by 8? Turn and talk with your partner.
(*Students notice that every other number on the 4s chart is a count by 8 number.*)

Caleb: You can just look at every other number—8, 16, 24, 32.

Ms. Brown: Why can you do that?

Caleb: Because two 4s make 8.
(*Ms. Brown asks students to think about the first three numbers and to signal when they know these numbers. The students begin the count. Some count while looking at the count by 4s for guidance. Ms. Brown stops them at 96.*)

Ms. Brown: Let's stop and talk about the patterns that are helping you figure out the next number. Turn and talk with your partner about the patterns that are helping you and how you know what number comes next. (*As partners talk, Ms. Brown listens in and considers which patterns should be shared.*)

Isabel: I used every other number on the 4s chart. But the numbers stopped at 80. So I added 8 more to make 88 and 8 more to make 96. Now I just add 8 more.

Evan: The numbers in the ones place is the same in each column: 8-8-8, 6-6-6. So I know that the next number will end in 4, and it will be 104.
(*Ms. Brown underlines the 8s and 6s in the first two columns, as many students signal their agreement.*)

Ms. Brown: Evan has explained that he knows the next number will have a 4 in the ones place. Does anyone else have a strategy to help us know the next number?

Taylor: You add 40 more for each row. See 8 plus 40 equals 48 and 48 plus 40 equals 88. (*Ms. Brown writes +40 and draw arrows.*) And 64 + 40 equals 104.
(*Ms. Brown asks whether everyone agrees and then continues the count beginning back at 64. The class continues the count and Ms. Brown stops them at 160. She asks them to look at the three choral counts and to talk with their partners about what the three counts have in common. [See Figure 5.8.] As she listens, she thinks about how she will move the class toward thinking about the relationship between these multiples.*)

Figure 5.8

Ms. Brown's class compares the patterns they notice among these three counts.

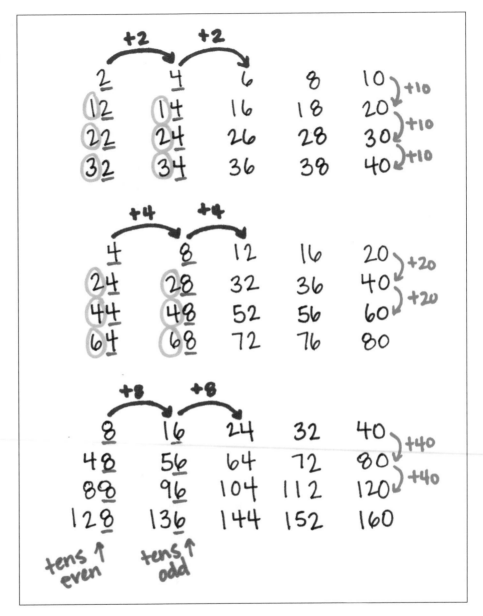

Franklin: All of the numbers are even.

Naima: There's a multiple of 10 at the end of each row.

Mohamad: Some of the numbers are on all three charts and some of the numbers aren't.

Ms. Brown: Which numbers are on all three charts?

Mohamad: 8, 16, 24, 32, 40.

(*Ms. Brown pauses the students' discussions to raise Mohamad's noticing: some numbers show up in all three counts. She asks partners to talk about which numbers appear in all three charts and why.*)

Elijah: All of the numbers are multiples of 2, 4, and 8. You land on them when you count by 2, 4, and 8.

Ms. Brown: If we kept Choral Counting, would all of the multiples of 8 also be a multiple of 2? Would it be a multiple of 4? How do you know? Turn and talk with your partner.

(*Ms. Brown chose this question to encourage her class to think about the multiplicative relationship between 2, 4, and 8.*)

Byron: I think multiples of 8 are also multiples of 2 because they are even numbers.

Munira: And multiples of 8 are also multiples of 4 because when you count by 4s every other number is a multiple of 8.

(*Students share a few more ideas and then Ms. Brown ends the count by summarizing what students have noticed about multiples of 2, 4, and 8.*)

Exploring Multiples of 10: Connecting Counting by 3 and 30

Mr. Peterson's third-grade class has been exploring multiplication and division of single-digit numbers, and they are ready to begin to think about multiplying by multiples of 10. Today, Mr. Peterson plans to connect yesterday's choral count by 3 with a choral count by 30. He anticipates that his students will use knowledge of multiplication *and* place value in their discussion about the two counts.

In yesterday's count, Mr. Peterson recorded the numbers in columns of 10, in order to highlight the repeating patterns in the ones place. In today's count, Mr. Peterson plans to use the same organization to help students notice the similarities between counting by 3 and counting by 30. He predicts that the students will notice that they are basically the same count, but the count by 30 has a zero appended to each number. He hopes to leverage these noticings to discuss the difference between counting by groups of 3 *ones* and groups of 3 *tens*.

As students counted by 3 yesterday, they noticed that each column increased by 30, and they concluded that "each column goes up by 30 because we are counting 3 ten times." Mr. Peterson hopes to extend this idea today as he encourages students to contemplate why each column increases by 300.

Let's join Mr. Peterson's class as they begin today's count. Mr. Peterson has hung the chart from yesterday's choral count by 3 and asked his students to talk with their partner about the patterns they noticed yesterday.

Mr. Peterson explains that they will be counting by 30 today. The class begins, pausing at 180 to discuss how they are figuring out the next number. Mr. Peterson stops the class at 720 and asks students to share the patterns they notice.

Miski: There's always a zero in the ones place.

Vlad: The number in the tens place is the same across each row. Like 3, 3, 3 and 6, 6, 6.

Alicia: The columns go up by 300: 30 plus 300 is 330 and 330 plus 300 is 630.
(*Mr. Peterson notates these ideas on the chart. Then he asks students to look for similarities between the two choral counts. See Figure 5.9.*)

Figure 5.9
Mr. Peterson's plan for related counts by 3 and 30.

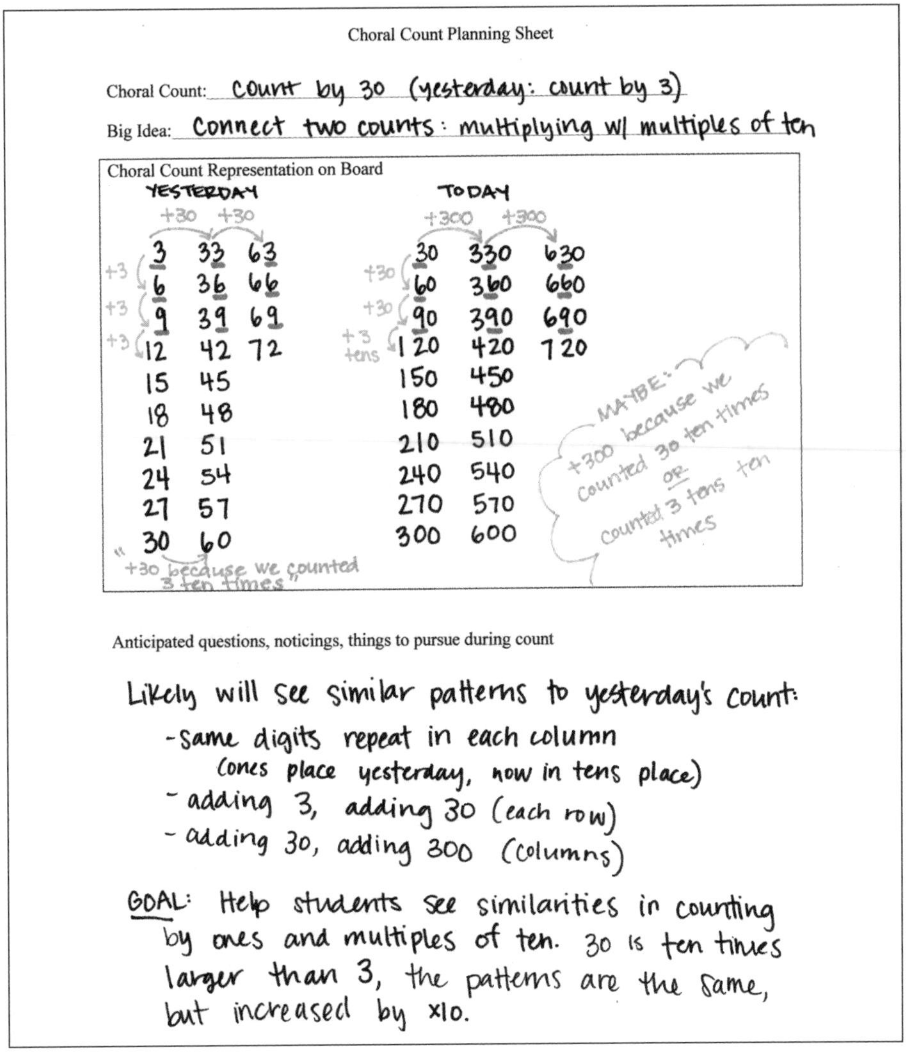

Choral Count Planning Sheet

Choral Count: **count by 30 (yesterday: count by 3)**

Big Idea: **Connect two counts: multiplying w/ multiples of ten**

Choral Count Representation on Board

YESTERDAY

	+30	+30
3	33	63
6	36	66
9	39	69
12	42	72
15	45	
18	48	
21	51	
24	54	
27	57	
30	60	

+3 (rows)

"+30 because we counted 3 ten times"

TODAY

	+300	+300
30	330	630
60	360	660
90	390	690
120	420	720
150	450	
180	480	
210	510	
240	540	
270	570	
300	600	

+30 +3 tens

MAYBE:
+300 because we counted 30 ten times
or
counted 3 tens ten times

Anticipated questions, noticings, things to pursue during count

Likely will see similar patterns to yesterday's count:
- same digits repeat in each column
  (ones place yesterday, now in tens place)
- adding 3, adding 30 (each row)
- adding 30, adding 300 (columns)

GOAL: Help students see similarities in counting by ones and multiples of ten. 30 is ten times larger than 3, the patterns are the same, but increased by ×10.

Zachary: The 30s chart is sort of like the 3s chart. I used the 3s to help me count by 30. On that chart (*pointing to the count-by-3 chart*) it goes 3, 6, 9, 12, and it goes 3, 6, 9, 12 over there, too (*pointing to the count-by-30 chart*). (*Students use their "I agree" signal to show that they saw the same pattern. Mr. Peterson has worked to orient his students to the ideas of their peers, by encouraging them to listen carefully and to show when they agree with others' ideas.*)

Mr. Peterson: Where do you see 3, 6, 9 in each chart?

Zachary, (*pointing to the chart*): There!

Mr. Peterson: What place are the digits in?

Zachary: The 3, 6, 9 is in the ones column on that chart (*pointing to the count-by-3 chart*), and they're in the tens on the other chart.

Mr. Peterson: Who can repeat what Zachary said?

(*Mr. Peterson calls on two students to repeat. As anticipated, the class used their choral count by 3 to support their count by 30. Mr. Peterson's follow-up question encouraged Zachary to use place value language to describe what he saw. By asking students to repeat Zachary's idea, Mr. Peterson provides multiple opportunities for students to describe what they see using place value language.*)

Mr. Peterson: So, a lot of you used the count-by-3 chart to count by 30. But why does it work? Why can we use the count by 3 to help us count by 30?

Liz: When we count by 30 we just add a zero to the number. Like we added a zero to 3 and a zero to 6.

Mr. Peterson: Hmm. I'm wondering about something. When I add a zero to a number, I get the same number. Like 9 plus zero equals 9. Did we *add* a zero in our count?

Nicole: No, we just put a zero on the end.

Mr. Peterson: So we're not adding zero to the number. When we put a zero in the ones place, we can say that we append or attach a zero. But, why does it work to just append a zero when we are counting by 30? Turn and talk with your partner about why you think that works.

(*Mr. Peterson listens in on the partner conversations to see how students are thinking about counting by groups of 1s versus counting by groups of 10s. He hears some students continue to talk about appending a zero, while others are beginning to describe the two counts using what they know about place value. He selects two of these students to begin the discussion.*)

Mr. Peterson: I heard lots of ideas about counting by 1s and counting by 10. Roberto, would you share what you're thinking?

Roberto: In that count (*pointing*), we were counting by three 1s. But in this count (*pointing*), we're counting by 10s.

Amiyah: And there's only 10s and no 1s.

(As Roberto shares, Mr. Peterson circles the 3s in the ones place in the first count and the 3s in the tens place in the second count. He underlines the zeros to highlight Amiyah's idea.)

Mr. Peterson: How does this help us understand why we can append a zero when we count by multiples of 10?

Yahyah: Because 30 is 10 times as big as 3 and there's no 1s.

(Mr. Peterson gives students time to revoice Yahyah's idea and then asks for any other similarities and differences between the count and gives students time to turn and talk. Students point to the charts as they talk.)

Smiti: When we count by 3s, the columns go up by 30, and when we count by 30, the columns go up by 300.

Mr. Peterson: Why?

Smiti: Well, we said that ten 3s make 30. Ten 30s make 300. And 300 is 10 times 30.

While either of these counts could be done independently to work toward a variety of mathematical goals, Mr. Peterson used them in tandem to make the multiples of 10 connection readily visible. The students quickly saw that they could count by 30 by using their previous count by 3 and placing a zero in the ones place. This provided students with an opportunity to explore what happens when you multiply a number by 10 and use the structure of place value to think about multiples of 10.

Big Mathematical Ideas Related to Multiplication and Division

Choral Counting involves counting multiples of a given factor, like 2, 4, 8, 3, 30, or any other number you can dream up. Counting by a single-digit number can support students to transition from counting by ones to skip-counting as they make use of patterns that repeat. For example, notice the patterns in this count by 9. (See Figure 5.10.) While some students may add 10 and take-away 1, students may also notice that the digit in the ones place decreases by 1, while the number in the tens place increases by one 10.

As we saw in the previous vignettes, connecting related counts supports students to see the multiplicative connection between factors and multiples. Counting by 2, 4, and 8, or 3, 6, and 9 can help students see these connections. As students connect single-digit counts with counts by multiples, they explore the difference between counting groups of 1 and groups of 10s, 100s, or 1,000s. Choral Counting by multiples of 10, 100, or 1,000 highlights the base 10

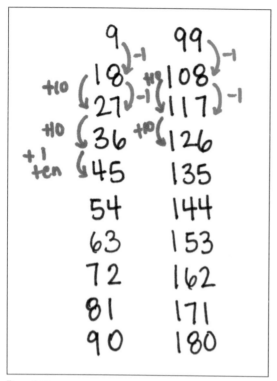

$$9 \;)_{-1} \qquad 99 \;)_{-1}$$

+10 $(18 \;)_{-1}$ +9 $(108 \;)_{-1}$
$(27 \;)_{-1}$ $(117 \;)_{-1}$

+10 $(36$ +10 $(126$
+1
ten $(45$ 135

54   144

63   153

72   162

81   171

90   180

Figure 5.10
Notice the patterns that emerge in a count by 9 starting at 9.

structure of numbers. This may support students' use of the base 10 structure to multiply two- and three-digit numbers.

Choral counts by two-digit numbers encourage students to develop a repertoire of computational strategies that rely on thinking flexibly about numbers and quantities. For example, to count multiples of 12, a student might break apart the number by place value, adding 10 plus 2 more. This may support students as they begin to use partial products to multiply two- and three-digit numbers.

Choral Counting forward and then backward may develop understanding of multiplication as repeated addition and division as repeated subtraction. The forward count scaffolds the backward count, which is more difficult. A forward count by 3 can be connected to multiplication by asking, *If you count by 3 eight times, what number would you say? How could we write this as an equation?* To connect a backward count with division you might ask, *When you start at 24, how many times do you have to count backward by 3 to get to zero?* A context, connected with a choral count, can help students think about using repeated subtraction as they "scoop" out equal groups. For example: *Sam baked 36 cookies. He put 4 in each bag for friends. How many bags did he fill?* With this context, you might ask students to count backward on a number line by 4, beginning at 36. After counting backward to zero, you might ask, "How many bags did Sam fill? How did you use the count to figure it out?" and represent their jumps back on the number line.

Choral Counting to Develop Ideas About Fractions and Decimals

In the primary grades, children need many opportunities to count with whole numbers to practice important counting sequences (e.g., counting by 1, 5, 10, 100) and to gain a sense of magnitude (e.g., how big is 100?). Similarly, students in the upper grades need many counting opportunities as they continue learning about new sets of numbers: fractions and decimals. Choral counts can be used to support students to develop conceptual understanding of fractions as numbers. With repeated exposure to counting by fractional amounts, students come to understand that fractions can describe quantities less than one, greater than one, and that there is often more than one way to describe a quantity. For example, 2 can also be described as $\frac{6}{3}$ or $\frac{2}{1}$. Counting by decimal amounts can help students connect fraction and decimal notation; for example, one-tenth can be written both as 0.1 and $\frac{1}{10}$. It can also support students' understanding of the relationships between whole numbers, tenths, hundredths, and thousandths within the base 10 system. Choral Counting can provide students with the opportunity to extend their understanding of operations with whole numbers to operations with fractions.

Counting by a Mixed Number: "If $4\frac{4}{4}$ is the same as 5, what number will we say next in our count?"

Ms. Moe's fourth-grade class has just started their fractions unit. Ms. Moe is curious about her students' understanding of fractions, mixed numbers, and equivalency. She has planned a choral count by $1\frac{1}{4}$ to surface these ideas. Based on a previous count by a unit fraction, Ms. Moe anticipates that her students will add one whole and a unit fraction with ease. She wants her students to think about what happens to the count when the $\frac{1}{4}$s make another whole.

Ms. Moe explains that they are going to count by $1\frac{1}{4}$ today and begins the count. Ms. Moe stops the class at $4\frac{4}{4}$ and, after giving them a couple of minutes to talk with their partners about the patterns they notice, she asks students to share.

Emi: The whole numbers go up by one.

Ahmed: The numerator goes up by one, but the denominator stays the same.

Ms. Moe: Why?

Ahmed: Because we're counting by fourth-sized pieces. The number of pieces goes up by one, but the size of the piece stays the same.

Isaac: We ended on $\frac{4}{4}$ and $\frac{4}{4}$ makes a whole. So we really have 5.

(*Ms. Moe asks a student to revoice this important idea, then she draws an area model showing the 4 wholes and $\frac{4}{4}$ that make another whole.*)

Ms. Moe: Like this, Isaac? (*He nods.*) If $4\frac{4}{4}$ is the same as 5, what number will we say next in our count?

Naomi: $6\frac{1}{4}$ because if you add 5 plus $1\frac{1}{4}$ you get $6\frac{1}{4}$.

(*Students signal that they agree and Ms. Moe starts the count again, beginning at $3\frac{3}{4}$. After $9\frac{4}{4}$, some students say $10\frac{1}{4}$, while others say $11\frac{1}{4}$. Ms. Moe stops the class to discuss which number will actually come next.*)

Ms. Moe: I heard students say different numbers. I heard $10\frac{1}{4}$ and $11\frac{1}{4}$. Talk with your partner about what number should come next and why.

(*As Ms. Moe listens to the partners talk, she hears many students quickly agreeing that the next number will be* $11\frac{1}{4}$. *She decides that this would be a good opportunity to normalize, and indeed celebrate, making errors and revising your thinking. She pulls the class back together and asks what number comes next.*)

Class: $11\frac{1}{4}$.

Ms. Moe: How do you know? Is there someone who revised their thinking who'd be willing to share?

Jacob: Well, at first I thought it was $10\frac{1}{4}$ because I added one whole to 9. But then my partner, Micah, said that $9\frac{4}{4}$ is the same as 10, so I needed to add $1\frac{1}{4}$ to 10. And that's $11\frac{1}{4}$.

Ms. Moe: Oh, I see just what you did there. Did anyone else have the same idea as Jacob at first?

(*Some students use a silent signal to show they had similarly revised their thinking. Ms. Moe restarts the count. This time, the class successfully counts past $14\frac{4}{4}$, and Ms. Moe stops the count at $19\frac{4}{4}$. She asks students to think about any new patterns they notice and then to share them with their partner.*)

Marion: It goes $\frac{1}{4}, \frac{1}{4}, \frac{1}{4}, \frac{1}{4}$ (pointing at the first row) and then $\frac{2}{4}$ (pointing at the second row) and then there's $\frac{3}{4}$ and then $\frac{4}{4}$.

(*Ms. Moe underlines the row of fourths to highlight Marion's idea.*)

Taylor: You're adding 5 more to each column: $1\frac{1}{4}$ plus 5 is $6\frac{1}{4}$. $6\frac{1}{4}$ plus 5 is $11\frac{1}{4}$.

(*Ms. Moe records this idea on the chart.*)

Ms. Moe: Why does every column increase by 5? Talk with your partner.

(*After a few minutes to talk, she asks students to share.*)

Katherine: In every column, we are counting 4 wholes and $\frac{4}{4}$, which makes 5 altogether. It's like Isaac's picture in red.

Carlos: 4 and $\frac{4}{4}$ equals 5. And $9\frac{4}{4}$ equals 10. And $14\frac{4}{4}$ equals 15. So it's going up by 5. (*See Figure 5.11.*)

Some of the other vignettes in this chapter depict choral counts with a specific, targeted math goal in mind. However, in this case, Ms. Moe used this discussion as an opportunity to listen to her students' current thinking about mixed numbers. She anticipated that her students would add $1\frac{1}{4}$ with ease but was curious about how they would transition to the next

Figure 5.11
Taylor notices that the numbers increase by 5 across the columns.

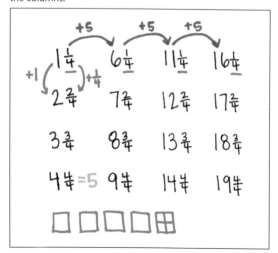

column. While choral counts can be used to serve a targeted mathematical goal, you might also use them in this more open ended, exploratory manner.

Notice that Ms. Moe selected a number that she thought would be accessible for students to count by. It's helpful to select numbers that you anticipate students having some success with. An overly complex count is likely to be frustrating and detract from your goal of analyzing the patterns that emerge from the count. If getting started seems challenging, you might ask students to think about the first three numbers in the count before beginning. Pausing early in the count to ask students to share strategies for finding the next number is another way to make sure all students can participate.

Big Mathematical Ideas Related to Fractions and Decimals

Counting fractional parts helps students see how parts relate to the whole. Counting by unit fractions (like $\frac{1}{4}, \frac{1}{2}, \frac{1}{5}$) supports students in understanding that the numerator tells how many pieces are being counted and the denominator tells the size of the pieces, or what is being counted. As students count by a non-unit fractional amount such as $\frac{3}{4}$, they think about counting a number of pieces that are a particular size, or 3 fourth-size pieces. They attend to patterns as the number of pieces grows, while the size of the piece remains constant. In these choral counts, students also think about how many of these pieces make a whole, developing the idea of equivalent fractions and mixed numbers.

Counting by a fraction enables students to extend their understanding of multiplication of whole numbers to multiplying fractions by whole numbers, as well as dividing a whole number by a fraction. For example, a class might use a choral count to think about the following measurement division problem: *Katie needs $\frac{3}{4}$ of a pound of clay to make a pot. How many pots can she make with 12 pounds of clay?*

Choral counts by decimals and decimal fractions (fractions with a denominator that is a power of 10, e.g., tenths, hundredths) on the same number line can help students make connections between fraction and decimal notation. They gain a deeper understanding of the numbers that exist *between* whole numbers on a number line as they count the hundredths between 2.6 and 2.7 and thousandths between 2.63 and 2.64. Counting by 0.01s (1.86, 1.87, 1.88, 1.89, 1.90) provides an opportunity for students to see how ten 0.01s make a new 0.1. Decimal choral counts by greater values than 1 provide students with the opportunity to combine whole numbers and decimal quantities. For example, in order to count by 1.9, students may recall counting by 19 and extend the base 10 pattern with whole numbers to decimals. Instead of adding 2 tens and subtracting 1, they can now add 2 wholes and subtract 0.1.

* * *

Trying Out Choral Counting in Your Classroom

Once you and your students are in the routine of Choral Counting, 15 minutes tends to be a good amount of time to do a little counting and notice some patterns. It may take you more time when you're first starting because you'll need to introduce the activity. If you find your that choral counts take 30 or more minutes regularly, consider your purpose. Are you spending a lot of time just getting the count out? Consider counting by numbers that are easier for students so you can get to the rich exploration of patterns. Are you spending a lot of time discussing the important mathematical ideas you want your students to be learning about? Great! But don't feel the need to squeeze every possible pattern out of the count in one day. You want to keep the joy and momentum alive. If you think there is a lot more good discussion to be had around the count, but that students' stamina is flagging, you can always return to a count another day. Save it and come back to it! (See Appendix 3 for more examples of teachers' experimentation with Choral Counting.)

Choral Counting is an invitation; it provides an opportunity for each student to generate important mathematical ideas and for teachers to be curious about their students' thinking. Choral Counting can be joyful but messy; the choral aspect of this activity means your students are likely to participate exuberantly, but they won't always know the next number. It is generative; new and interesting or confusing ideas will emerge in Choral Counting which can act as a springboard for further conversation.

Choral Counting Examples to Try in the Upper Grades		
Counts	**Mathematical Ideas**	**Examples**
Counts with whole numbers		
Forward and backward by multiples of 10 or 100	• Patterns in the base 10 number system exist, regardless of the starting point of the count • Counting by multiples of 100 fluently • Connect ideas about groups of 1s, 10s, and 100s	See "Choral Counting with Whole Numbers: Exploring Place Value" (p. 115) See "Exploring Multiples of 10: Connecting Counting by 3 and 30" (p. 128)
Forward by a single digit	• Patterns when skip-counting • Repeated addition • Multiplication	See "Relating Multiple Counts: Are Multiples of 8 Also Multiples of 4 and Multiples of 2? Why?" (p. 124)

Forward by connected factors - by 2, 4, 8 - by 3, 6 - by 6, 12	• Doubling and halving • Multiplicative relationships	See "Relating Multiple Counts: Are Multiples of 8 Also Multiples of 4 and Multiples of 2? Why?" (p. 124)
Forward by a two-digit number - by 11 - by 12 - by 15 - by 19 - by 21	• Repeated addition • Multiplication • Patterns in the base 10 number system	Count by 19
Backward by a single digit	• Repeated subtraction • Measurement division • Patterns when skip-counting	Count backward by 4 beginning at 100

(continued)

| Backward by a two-digit number
- by 15
- by 21 | • Repeated subtraction
• Measurement division
• Patterns in the base 10 number system | Count by backward 21 (with or without a context)

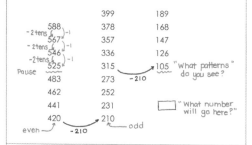 |

Patterns you expect to be noticed and responses or extension questions you might ask:

- Digit in the ones place decreases by 1 (8, 7, 6, 5...)
- Digit in the tens place decreases by 2 (8, 6, 4, 2)
- Digit in the hundreds place repeats five times, then four times.
- If you look at the tens and hundreds places, the tens decrease by 2 tens (58 tens, 56 tens, 54 tens, ...)
- The numbers in the tens place are even in the first column, then odd in the second column.
- Each column increases by 210. – *Why do the columns increase by 210?*

Choral counting with fractions, mixed numbers, and decimals

| Forward by unit fractions | • Meaning of fractions
• Fractions can be greater than 1
• Equivalence | Count by $\frac{1}{4}$ (with or without a context)

Count: by $\frac{1}{4}$
Context: Maria ran ¼ of a mile every day for 2 weeks. How many miles did she run altogether?

Anticipated Counting Strategy
Increase the numerator by 1, while keeping the denominator the same.

Record of Count and Patterns:

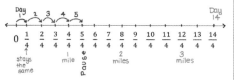 |

Notes (pauses, questions, anticipated student responses)

Pause at $\frac{5}{4}$

- What patterns do you notice?
  The number of pieces (numerator) increases by 1.
  The size of the piece (denominator) stays the same.
- Why does the size of the piece (denominator) stay the same?
- How many days has Maria run?
- How far has Maria run so far?
  1 ¼ miles because 4/4 is equal to one mile plus 1 more fourth.

Stop at 14/4

- How many miles did Maria run? How do you know?

Forward by non-unit fractions	• Multiply fractions
	• Determine equivalent fractions
		Count by $\frac{2}{3}$ (with or without a context)
		
		Count: by $\frac{2}{3}$
		
		Context: I want to bake a cake and I need $6\frac{2}{3}$ cup of flour. But I only have a $\frac{2}{3}$ sized measuring cup. Let's count by $\frac{2}{3}$ to see how many scoops I need.
		
		Anticipated Counting Strategy
		Increase the numerator by 2, while keeping the denominator the same.
		
		Record of Count and Patterns:
		
		+2 third size pieces
		+2
		
		$\frac{2}{3}$ $\frac{4}{3}$ $\frac{6}{3}$ $\frac{8}{3}$ $\frac{10}{3}$ $\frac{12}{3}$ $\frac{14}{3}$ $\frac{16}{3}$ $\frac{18}{3}$ $\frac{20}{3}$ "Stop!"
		
		Pause
		
		stays the same
		2 cups
		4 cups
		6 cups
		
		$\frac{3}{3}=1$ $\frac{6}{3}=2$
		
		Notes (pauses, questions, anticipated student responses)
		Pause at $\frac{12}{3}$
		- What patterns do you notice?
		   The number of pieces (numerator) increases by 2.
		   The size of the piece (denominator) stays the same.
		- Why does the size of the piece (denominator) stay the same?
		- How much have we counted so far? How do you know?
		- We're going to keep counting. Say "Stop" when you think we've reached 6 2/3.
		At $\frac{20}{3}$ students will say "Stop".
		
		- How do you know that we have $6\frac{2}{3}$ cups of flour?

Forward by mixed numbers	• Repeated addition of mixed numbers • Multiply fractions	See "Counting by a Mixed Number: If $4\frac{4}{4}$ is the same as 5, what number will we say next in our count?" (p. 133)
Forward by decimal numbers (tenths, hundredths, thousandths)	• Decimal patterns in the base 10 number system. • Patterns in the placement of the decimal point when a decimal is multiplied or divided by a power of 10	Count by 0.1 from 2.32 **Count:** by .1 (one tenth) from 2.32 **Anticipated Counting Strategy** Increase the digit in the tenths by 1. Add 1 tenth. (22 tenths, 23 tenths, 24 tenths...) **Record of Count and Patterns:** 3.02 4.02 +.1 3.12 4.12 3.22 4.22 2.32 +1 whole 3.32 +1 whole 4.32 +.1 2.42 3.42 4.42 +.1 2.52 3.52 4.52 What patterns do you see? 2.62 3.62 2.72 3.72 2.82 3.82 2.92 3.92 Pause What number comes next? How do you know? What number will go here? Patterns you expect to be noticed and responses / extension questions you might ask: - The digit in the hundredths place remains the same. - The digit in the ones place remains the same in a column. - The digit in the tenths place increases by 1 (1 tenth) until you get to .9. Then the digit in the tenths place returns to 0. *Why?* - The digit in the tenths place repeats across the columns. - The columns increase by 1. *Why do the columns increase by 1 whole?* - The first two digits begin at "23" and increase by 1. "23, 24, 25" *What's increasing? Oh, it's increasing by a tenth. Let's count... 23 tenths and 2 hundredths, 24 tenths and 2 hundredths, 25 tenths and 2 hundredths...*

(continued)

Money	• Decimal patterns in the base 10 number system.	Count by $1.25 Count by $0.75

Counts with units of measure

By minutes or hours	• Elapsed time • 60 minutes in an hour	Count by 5 minutes. *Context: The movie starts at 11:40 and lasts 1 hour and 35 minutes. What time will it end?*
By inches or feet	Length conversion	Count by 4 inches

Count: Forward by 4 inches	**Anticipated Counting Strategy**
Mrs. Wong needs 4 inches of ribbon to make a bow. She wants to use 2 yards of ribbon and save the rest for later. How many bows can she make with two yards?	Count up 4. Add 20 to the number in the previous column.

Record of Count and Patterns:

```
      4"      24" 2ft.   44"        64"
+4?   8"      28"        48" 4ft.   68"
     12" 1ft. 32"        52"        72" 6ft.
     16"      36" 3ft.   56"
                  1yd.
     20"      40"        60" 5ft.
            +20"      +20"
```

Patterns you expect to be noticed and responses or extension questions you might ask:
- The digits in the ones repeats across the columns.
- The pattern in the ones place repeats (4, 8. 2, 6, 0, 4, 8. 2, 6, 0...)
- Each column increases by 20.
- Three "four inches" equals one foot.

After 24 inches ask "How do you know the next number?" "Are we close to 2 yards? How much have we counted so far"

After 48 inches ask for two or three patterns. Then ask "How much have we counted? Remember to say stop when we get to 2 yards."

After students say "stop" at 76 inches ask "How do you know that this is two yards?"

Return to the context and ask, "How many bows can Mrs. Wong make?"

CHAPTER 6

Preschool Connections

by Nick Johnson and Natali Gaxiola

The children in Ms. Lupe's four-year-old class are Counting Collections during small-group time. As they sit down at the kidney table, their teacher hands each child a bag of objects. Each collection bag is filled with different objects—one has colored popsicle sticks inside, another a set of small rocks found at the beach, and another a set of old used keys brought in by students. Most of the collections contain a range of 12–20 items, although the teacher has purposely given Camilo a collection of 35 wooden cubes and Matthew a collection of 8 colored plastic dinosaurs.

The children are familiar with the routine, and most immediately dive into the activity. Even though it is only October, they have been Counting Collections regularly since the middle of August when they started preschool. The children begin in different ways, but they are all excited to get started with their collections. Aileen begins counting out loud as she takes her rocks out of the bag, one at a time. Andres dumps out his entire bag of toy animals and begins standing them up. As Susie empties her bag of pennies, several fall onto the floor. She picks them up (overlooking one) and then proceeds to line up her pennies in a row. She does not begin counting until she is satisfied with how they are all lined up.

Ms. Lupe watches closely as the children at her table begin working with their collections, observing the details of what her students do and say. (See Figure 6.1.) She hears Aileen count, "1, 2, 3, 4, 7, 8, 9, 10 . . ." as she takes her rocks out of the bag and notes that Aileen says exactly one number word for each object. Marcus has not started counting his popsicle sticks yet; he is sorting them by color. Julia tells her teacher that she has 14 milk caps. Ms. Lupe asks,

Figure 6.1
Counting
Collections during
small-group time.

"Can I hear you count them again?" and Julia counts, "1, 2, 3, 4, 5, 6, 7, 8, 9, 10, 11, 12, 14." Ms. Lupe responds, "So how many caps are in your collection?" "14!" says Julia.

Continued experiences like these will allow Ms. Lupe's students to connect their curiosity and rich informal understandings about the world around them to the mathematics of school. Providing regular opportunities to count collections will support children not only to build a strong foundation in counting, but also to connect and extend their knowledge of counting to other important mathematics in early childhood. In this chapter we describe how Counting Collections can support the development of young children's mathematical thinking. We will also provide examples of how teachers have used Counting Collections in their classrooms to learn about and extend their students' mathematical understanding.

Counting Collections in Preschool

Counting has long been a part of children's preschool experiences. Children chant the number sequence out loud to 10, count how tall their block tower is, show how old they are using their fingers, and so on. Counting a set of objects may appear to be a simple task to adults, but preschool teachers recognize that the intricacies of learning to count are challenging and complex for young children. Preschoolers need time and varied opportunities across a range of settings to develop their understanding of counting. Fortunately, children show remarkable intuitive understandings of the principled ideas that allow us to count (Carpenter et al. 2017). Providing regular opportunities for your preschoolers to count collections will support their developing understanding of counting and attending to the details of how they count will allow you as a teacher to build from what they know. Counting Collections can also provide a space for young children to begin to develop identities as knowers and doers of mathematics, and to experience school mathematics as a place where their ideas are valued and make sense.

Learning how to count involves the coordination of three principled ideas: (1) there is an ordered sequence of number names, (2) counting involves assigning exactly one number name to each object, and (3) the last number used when counting provides the total quantity of the set.* These ideas do not necessarily develop in a particular order for children. For example, one child may display a strong grasp of one-to-one correspondence but still skip some number names when counting, while another child may count out loud accurately from 1–10 but not match each counting word with an object. Yet another child might count 8 objects with one-to-one correspondence using the standard 1–8 number sequence, but when asked how many are in the collection respond, "a lot," or recount the collection rather than responding "8."

Developing an understanding of what counting *is* involves using these principles in relation to each other. Providing regular opportunities for children to count objects allows them to engage with ideas of one-to-one correspondence, the counting sequence, and cardinality together, supporting their mutual development. While most children entering preschool do not demonstrate consistent, accurate use of all of the counting principles, all children will show some understanding as they begin to count collections. Allowing children to organize objects for themselves, to sort their collection any way they like (for example, by color or size), or inviting them to count their collection again or in a different way can support their engagement with the counting principles and allow them to count in ways that make sense to them.

---

*Gelman and Gallistel (1986) refer to the three *how to count* principles as (1) the stable-order principle, (2) the one-to-one principle, and (3) the cardinal principle and show how young children often display understanding of these principles even before they are consistent in applying them accurately.

Learning to Count

Counting Sequence
There is an ordered sequence of number names. Counting involves using the same sequence each time, starting with 1. Extending the counting sequence involves making sense of the patterns of the base 10 number system.

One-to-One Correspondence
Exactly one number from the counting sequence is assigned to each object in the collection.

Cardinality
The last number assigned to an object in counting the collection represents the total quantity of the collection.

Getting Started

Children enter preschool eager to explore the classroom world that surrounds them. They are captivated by a new environment filled with things they may have never seen or experienced before. Counting Collections can provide a way to build on their interests and enthusiasm while tapping into the knowledge they bring with them into school. In preparing collections to begin the school year, many teachers create collections from items that are already part of the classroom environment. Others invite children to bring in collections from home to share with the class or to build collections from things like milk caps that are part of children's daily lives. Counting Collections can take place across a variety of classroom settings and spaces. Some teachers, such as Ms. Lupe, find that small-group time works well for Counting Collections. Other teachers find it useful to engage the entire class in the activity, circulating and dropping in on students as they count. Still others choose to get started by inviting a single student to count a collection during choice time. We encourage you to try out Counting Collections in a way that makes sense to you and complements what you are already doing. In getting started, you might think about three goals: (1) to help children understand what the activity is all about, (2) to begin to learn what each child knows about counting, and (3) to make sure that the activity is enjoyable and that children feel successful.

During their first few experiences with Counting Collections, young children often need support to understand the activity's expectations—to know what they are supposed to do. A teacher might hand a child a collection (for example, of birthday candles) and ask, *How many candles do you have in your collection?* or *Can you count these birthday candles?* Other teachers might begin with more open-ended questions, *What do you notice about your collection?* or *What could we do with these candles?* or *Can you tell me about the collection you have?* Many children will need time to explore and engage with the objects in their collection, but the idea is (at some point) for the child to attempt to count their collection in a way that makes sense to them and for you as a teacher to observe and listen to the details of what they say and do.

While engaging children in counting, keep the activity fun and get children talking about their collections. Providing opportunities to discuss what each collection consists of also allows the children to satisfy their initial curiosity about the materials. As you observe children exploring, sorting, or organizing their collection, you can help them see that these are productive ways of engaging in the task. Asking simple questions based on what children do, or describing what you notice them doing, can help get children talking and support them to connect what they know about the objects with productive mathematical ideas. For example, if the child has sorted a collection of fuzzy pom-poms by size or by color, you might say, *Tell me about what you did with your collection,* or *I noticed you put these pom-poms together. Can you tell me about how you decided which ones to put together?* In classrooms we have worked in, teachers let children take the lead in what they do with their collections and how they decide to count.

Providing space for children to explore what they can do with their collections, both before, during, and after they have counted, can help the activity to remain inviting, enjoyable, and creative. Children will sort, organize, and work with their collections in a variety of ways. Some may slide objects over as they count. Others may place their objects into a line or stand up their objects as they count. As children are playing with the objects they are often playing with important mathematics. Some may organize their objects into patterns or reorganize an already-counted collection in a different way and count again. Finishing with the activity will not mean the same thing or look the same way for each child. For one child, it may be merely sorting their objects or counting only a part of their collection (for example, only the blue ones). For another, it may mean counting their objects back into the bag as they put them away or combining their collection with their neighbor's and counting the new, bigger collection. These children are all learning. We know one child who, in play after he had already counted, reorganized a collection of 12 keys into 3 equal groups of 4 keys! In watching and listening to what they do, children will show you what they understand not only about counting but also about other powerful mathematical ideas.

Representing Counting

Many teachers find it helpful to ask children to record or represent on paper how they have counted their collection. Some teachers prefer to introduce this part of the activity after children have had some experience counting, while others include representing the count as part of the activity from the beginning. Getting started can be as simple as asking the child: *Can you show on your paper how you counted your collection?* or *I'm going to give you a piece of paper. Can you draw your collection on it for me?* You might even choose to incorporate the word "representation:" *Can you represent your collection on this paper? Can you draw it?* Children will come up with various ways to begin to represent their collections. Some children will place their objects on the paper and attempt to trace them. Others will make a mark or circle on the paper and then place the object on top of it. Still others will try to draw the object itself. Eventually, some may even begin to incorporate numerals. (See Figures 6.2-6.4 for some common approaches children use in beginning to represent their collections.) Once children begin to catch on to what it means to show their collection on paper, they will often watch one another and pick up one another's ideas about how they can represent their counting.

Figure 6.2
Vanity draws a circle on her paper and places a popsicle stick on top of it until all of her sticks are on the paper.

Figure 6.3
Jayden slides over a key and makes a mark on his paper, one at a time, until each key has been represented.

Figure 6.4
Kailea places her collection of keys on her paper and begins to trace each one, removing the key once it has been traced.

Of course, what preschoolers show on their paper will vary a great deal, especially as they're getting started. Representing a particular quantity of concrete objects on paper can be quite an abstract idea for young minds to grapple with. After all, a drawing or mark on a paper is not the same thing as the object itself. It takes time for children to come to understand that while a representation may differ from the actual collection in many ways, what is important is for the quantity or amount represented to be the same. No matter how the child chooses to represent his or her collection, it can be productive to engage with the child around their representation or to support them to reflect on what they've done. For example, you might ask the child to tell you about what they've shown on their paper, invite them to count what they've drawn, or point to one part of their representation and ask them about it. Language development is a central goal of preschool and engaging with children about their collections and representations can provide a useful space to elicit children's ideas and to build connections between mathematics and literacy. Representing their collection also supports the development of spatial relations as children work to figure out how to manage the available space on the paper to "fit" their collection.

Supporting Children's Participation

Focusing on What Children Can Do

Children's participation and learning are supported by first focusing on what they know and can do. Attending to the details of what children say and do as they count often reveals that they know more about counting than might first be apparent. Rather than demonstrating to students how to count, many preschool teachers we work with concentrate first on simply listening and observing their students. This helps them to recognize the informal and intuitive understandings that children bring with them into school and to see that each child knows something about counting.

For example, early in the school year Ms. Torres noticed Hector counting a small collection of 7 plastic spoons. Hector lined up his spoons and counted, "1, 2, 4, 5, 7, 8, 9." A few minutes later he counted his spoons again and used the same sequence, "1, 2, 4, 5, 7, 8, 9." At first glance, it might appear that Hector has counted incorrectly. However, understanding the counting principles and attending to the details of how Hector counted allowed Ms. Torres to learn two things about Hector's counting on this day: (1) he used exactly one number word for each object, and (2) he used the same ordered sequence of number names each time. While Hector is still learning the "standard" counting sequence, on this day he demonstrated understanding of both the one-to-one principle as well as the principle that the counting sequence is used in the same order each time. Noting this, Ms. Torres decided to respond by explicitly recognizing what Hector knows.

"I noticed you counted each spoon and used the same numbers both times. Nice counting!" Ms. Torres knows that in the future she will provide other opportunities for Hector to learn the conventional counting sequence, perhaps by counting together with him or inviting him to count his collection with another student. On this day, however, she decided to focus her response on what he knows about counting. For Ms. Torres, it is important that each child feel successful in participating in the activity and that her responses build on the child's emergent understanding.

Responding to the Child's Existing Understanding

The details of children's counting can often provide teachers with ideas for ways to support their learning. In Ms. Maria's three-year-old classroom, Lesieli is counting a collection of 14 colored pencils. As Lesieli counts, she tries to touch each pencil, but the pencils are spaced closely together and a few do not get counted. Noticing this, Ms. Maria asks Lesieli if it would help to count her pencils again as she puts them back into the box. Lesieli likes this idea and tries it out, this time counting all 14 pencils with consistent one-to-one correspondence as she places them one at a time into the box. Ms. Maria knows that Lesieli sometimes has trouble keeping track of which objects have been counted and responded by reminding Lesieli of a strategy she had seen her use on a previous day.

Nearby Alonzo is counting a collection of 8 toy cars. He lines up his cars and counts 1–8. His teacher asks, "How many cars do you have, Alonzo?" and Alonzo recounts his collection, "1, 2, 3, 4, 5, 6, 7, 8." Ms. Maria again asks, "How many cars?" and rather than saying "8," Alonzo again recounts his collection. His teacher sees that Alonzo is still working on making sense of the relationship between counting and cardinality (that the last number in his count tells him that there are 8 cars in his collection) and adapts the task to see whether Alonzo can start with a given amount and create a collection of that size. She asks, "Alonzo, could you give me three of your cars?" Alonzo then counts out 3 cars into his teacher's hand—1, 2, 3. Ms. Maria replies excitedly, "You gave me three cars! Thank you, Alonzo!"

Even as children's accuracy is still emerging, their counting will reveal understanding that, once recognized, can be built upon. Back in Ms. Lupe's classroom, Camilo counts a collection of 35 colored wooden cubes, sliding each cube across the table as he counts out loud. His teacher notices that Camilo struggles a bit with the teen numbers when counting but that once he reaches 20 he uses a consistent, accurate sequence. Because he has skipped a few numbers in the teens, he arrives at a final count of 38. Ms. Lupe recognizes that although he is still learning the teen numbers, Camilo's counting beyond 20 reveals that he understands something about the patterns and structure of the number system, and she is curious to see whether he will extend these ideas into the forties. She adds a handful of cubes to his collection and asks Camilo if he can figure out how many cubes he has now. Camilo recounts his collection from one, again skips a few teen numbers, but beyond 20 uses the decade names and the recurring one to nine sequence to successfully count to 47! Rather than focusing on the teen numbers (which she knows can be difficult for children because of their irregular naming scheme), Ms. Lupe instead chose to build on what Camilo showed he understood about the base 10 number system. She knows that there will be many other opportunities (counting the children in line, counting out loud as they wash hands) for Camilo to continue to work on learning the teen numbers.

Supporting the Development of Children's Representations

Like with counting, children will bring different strengths to the task of representing their count, and each child will participate in his or her own unique way. For some, recording their count will be a challenge, while for others it will come with ease. Representing the entire collection may feel like an overwhelming task to some children. A teacher might scaffold the task of representing by asking, *Can you draw this one for me first?* or *For today how about we just show the blue ones?* It is not necessary for the child to produce a complete, accurate representation in order for learning to take place. Over time, children's representations will grow and become more mathematical in nature. The teachers we have worked with recognize that children's mathematical understandings are emerging alongside their language, fine-motor skills, and social-emotional development and find ways to support each child to be successful with what he or she is able to do on a given day. As you get to know your students and watch them begin to create representations, you will know when it makes sense to nudge them for a bit more and when to back off and let them be.

Once they are done (or as they are in the process of) representing it can be useful to have children reflect on what they have created. You can ask them to tell you about what they have done, or pick something on their paper and ask a question about it. For young children, the quantity represented on paper will often differ from the amount of objects in the actual collection. This can be a great opportunity to invite children to count what is on their paper and then to recount their collection (see Figures 6.5 and 6.6). Even if a representation is unclear to you (for example, the child produces something that resembles a scribble), you might say, *Tell me about what you made on your paper* or point to one of the objects in the collection and ask, *Can you show me where this one is in your drawing?* or *How could we show this one?* You can also support children to connect their representations with objects by offering language to describe what you observe the child doing. For example, *I see you drew a circle and then put the block on top of it* or *I noticed that each time you finish tracing a penny you take it off your paper and put it over here. What a lovely idea!* These observations can also provide a good starting point for follow-up questions—you can state what you just saw the child do and ask about it. Noticing, describing, and asking about the productive things you see children doing can be helpful both for the child who is performing that action as well as other children who are listening

Figure 6.5
Matthias represents his collection of 8 dinosaurs by making "a lot" of circles on his paper.

Figure 6.6
Rosie draws squeezer tops on her paper. Rosie's teacher asks her to recount her collection of tops and then to count what she has drawn on her paper. Seeing that she has too many on her paper, Rosie decides to cross out "the extra ones."

to and observing what is going on within the group. Children may pick up on a strategy that another child was using or simply reflect on their own work as they listen to the questions being posed to another classmate.

Developing Representations over Time

Given regular opportunities and support, preschoolers will display amazing progress in their ability to represent their counting on paper. Figures 6.7–6.18 show how two students' representations of counting progressed over the course of a school year.

Hailey (three years old) began the year making dots and lines on her paper (see Figure 6.7), but the idea that her representation should be connected to the

Figure 6.7

Figure 6.8

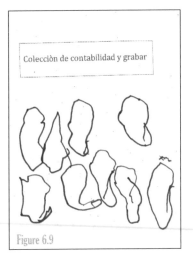

Figure 6.9

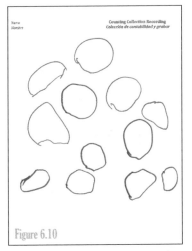

Figure 6.10

Figure 6.11b

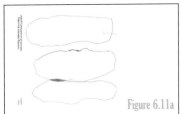

Figure 6.11a

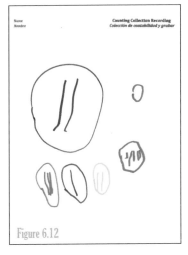

Figure 6.12

Hailey's progression in representing her counting across a school year.

objects in her collection was still emerging. Over time, she began to trace the objects on her paper and eventually to have the number of objects represented match the number of objects in the collection, even as she was still learning the number names beyond ten (Figures 6.8–6.10). Later in the school year, she began to use marks to represent objects rather than tracing the objects themselves, but this was a gradual process. For example, in the Figure 6.11, Hailey had counted a collection of 18 spoons. She ran out of room tracing spoons on the front of her paper and decided to continue on the back. When she also ran out of room on the back, she shifted to using marks to represent the remaining 12 items. However, when her teacher asked her to recount what she had represented on her paper, Hailey only counted the 6 large circles that had enclosed

Figure 6.13

Figure 6.14

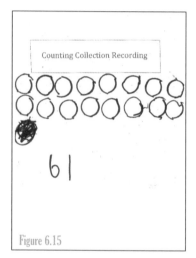

Figure 6.15

Figure 6.16

Figure 6.17

Figure 6.18

Jasmine's progression in representing her counting across a school year.

spoons; she did not count the additional marks. At this point for Hailey, the idea that a mark could stand for a spoon was still emerging. By the end of the year, Hailey was able to use marks to show on her paper how she had grouped her collection of 13 popsicle sticks by color (Figure 6.12).

Jasmine (four years old) also progressed a great deal throughout the year in her ability to represent her counting (see Figures 6.13–6.18). She began by drawing the objects themselves (her 6 buttons in Figure 6.13) and then began to trace the objects on her paper, later beginning to use some numerals (Figures 6.14–6.16). As her ability to represent progressed, she was encouraged to reflect on the relationship between the number of objects in her collection and the amount she had represented. For example, in recounting her representation in Figure 6.15, she noticed that she had traced one penny too many and crossed out the last penny on her paper (note also her reversal of the digits in writing 16). Later in the school year, she began to use lines (Figure 6.17) to represent objects rather than drawing or tracing them. By the end of the year, her representation showed not only groupings of objects (by color), but also the beginnings of number sentences related to the amounts in each group and the total amount of the collection (Figure 6.18). Not all preschoolers will be ready to begin to write number sentences, but Jasmine shows us what is possible when young children are provided ongoing opportunities to count collections and supported to represent their counts in ways that make sense to them.

Fostering Connections Between Home, School, and the Community

Parents and caregivers are helpful partners in learning about and supporting children's developing mathematical understanding. Sharing a story about something a child did and what it shows he or she knows about counting can be a great way to open a dialogue. What parents don't want to hear a story about how brilliant their child is! Talking with families can also provide you with a window into other ways that young children engage in mathematics outside of school; you may discover more about who a child is, his or her interests and experiences, and ways that you might build connections to what he or she already knows and can do. Many children enter preschool able to communicate in multiple languages. For example, parents may have supported their child to learn to count in English while speaking another language at home. A child may therefore be able to count a collection in English but need follow-up questions to be posed in his or her home language. Parents and caregivers can provide valuable insights on how to draw on a child's strengths and to surface mathematical understanding that may not be immediately apparent.

Teachers and parents can also share ideas about how to leverage the mathematical opportunities in everyday activities. For example, children can count out loud to 20 as they wash their hands or use the microwave timer to count down as they brush their teeth. Setting the table can be an activity that further develops one-to-one correspondence—the child can place one utensil with each plate, so that each person will have one. Or children can work on sorting, matching, and classifying by helping with laundry. A goal is to keep the mathematics playful while also being intentional. Having a number hunt or playing *I Spy* around the home or on a trip to the grocery store or counting the stairs on the playground up to the slide or finding the number of buttons that have to be snapped on a coat are just a few examples of ways to invite children to recognize the mathematics that surrounds us all and is a part of our daily lives. See Chapter 7 for more ideas on how to build connections and partnerships with families.

Adapt, Innovate, and Listen to Children

We continue to be excited and amazed by the ways that teachers adapt and innovate their classroom practice to build on their students' mathematical thinking. Here, we share just some of the ways that teachers have used the activity of Counting Collections to learn about children's ideas and to extend their mathematical opportunities. As you read, we encourage you to think about when and how these ideas might be productive for your students, and what you would want to think about in supporting children to engage with these ideas in ways that make sense to them.

- **Count larger collections.** We often learn a great deal about children's understanding by challenging them and then observing what they do as they try and make sense of a new situation. We sometimes see children able to count much larger collections than we would expect in preschool. And even as a child is still learning how to extend the number sequence, a larger collection may provide an opportunity for the child to organize or keep track of his or her count in a different way or for you to see what he or she understands about the underlying structure of the base 10 number system.
- **Count different kinds of objects.** Many children will count differently depending on what it is they are counting. They may slide their milk caps across the table to keep track but stand up each bear. They may sort toy animals by color but dinosaurs by the kind of dinosaur. Larger objects may create interesting challenges for students to represent. For example, if a child likes to place each object on top of his or her paper, a collection of spoons may not fit. A child might require a larger piece of paper or he or

she might move away from tracing and represent in a more abstract way. A collection of straws might be recorded by drawing lines that resemble tally marks, but a collection of pennies might be more likely to be represented using circles. Different objects provide different opportunities; making sure that children are given chances to count a variety of kinds of objects will give you a more complete picture of what they know and can do.

- **Make tools available.** Many children find using tools such as cups, trays, bowls, or felt counting mats can be helpful for sorting or organizing their collections, or for keeping track of which items have been counted. Some teachers choose to make tools available to children from the beginning, while others hold off until children ask for them or until the teacher notices a specific opportunity or need arise. Tools will often influence how children count their collections; we encourage you to introduce them when it seems appropriate and to consider taking them away from time to time to see what happens. Tools that involve numerals, such as a number chart or sentence strip with numbers on it, can help children to connect the numbers they are saying with the corresponding numeral. Many children will use these tools by starting at 1 and counting the numerals on the tool until they get to their number, so it is important for these tools be close by so that they can be touched and counted. The materials made available to children as they attempt to represent their counting will also influence what they do. Some children may benefit from the option of using multiple colors in drawing and representing, while others may be nudged to focus on quantity when only a single color is made available. A smaller piece of paper may push a child to think of a new way of representing his or her collection when the objects don't fit on top of the paper, while a larger paper may offer other possibilities.

- **Estimate.** Consider occasionally asking the child to make an estimate or guess about how many are in their collection before they count. The goal is not to guess correctly but, rather, to begin to think about the magnitude of numbers. Is a small bag of erasers about 10? About 25? About 100? Over time children will get better at guessing "about how many" they have. (See Figure 6.19.)

- **Invite students to engage with one another around counting.** It can be productive to ask children to count a collection together, to notice someone else's counting, or to compare their collections with one another. Negotiating how a pair will count together, finding whose collection has more, or figuring out why you and your partner do not arrive at the same amount when you count the same collection can provide both mathematical as well as social-emotional learning opportunities.

Figure 6.19
Ms. Lupe's students
think about how
many blocks are in
the collection.

Figure 6.19
Ms. Lupe's students think about how many blocks are in the collection.

- **Extend counting to solve problems.** A collection can provide a context for problem solving. Once the child has counted, you might offer a story about the collection in which something happens. A collection of 8 seashells could be added to (*If you found 4 more shells, how many would you have then?*), taken away from (*What if 3 shells got lost?*), or compared (*Do you have more round shells or pointy shells? How many more?*). A collection of 12 pennies could be used to buy candies that cost 3 pennies each or be shared between 4 people. We could wonder how many wheels are in a collection of 6 toy cars. Children enjoy making up their own stories about their collections, too! Research has demonstrated that children naturally model the actions and relationships within story situations and that children are able to solve a wide variety of problems without formal instruction in what we as adults recognize as addition, subtraction, multiplication, and division (Carpenter et al. 2017). Extending counting into problem solving can provide a way for children to begin to make sense of how the mathematical operations are connected to what they already know about stories, the world, and how it works.
- **Watch and listen for counting to emerge in informal spaces.** Counting is not something that only happens in school. Counting surrounds us and the world that we live in. Notice when and where young children count as

they live, as they play, as they make sense of the world around them. It is not always necessary to emphasize or follow up on the mathematics that emerges; it is often enough just to notice, appreciate, or marvel at the joy and brilliance of young people.

Letting Children Lead

Our goal here has been to illustrate some ways that teachers have used Counting Collections with preschoolers and to offer some big ideas about children's learning that can support your instructional decision making. There is no one or best way of using Counting Collections with young children. What is important is to find a way to get started that makes sense for you, to watch and listen to your students, and to reflect on your practice.

As they count collections, young children will show you what they know, and, over time, you will learn to recognize and build on their emerging understandings. We often want to jump in and show children how to count, to make sure they use the "correct" number sequence, or to make them organize in the way that makes sense to us as adults. But children do not always think about mathematics like we do. Learning with understanding takes time and often the process is as important (if not more so) than the outcome. Supporting learning often means creating space for children's partial understandings to emerge and recognizing the productive aspects of children's intuitive ideas and sense making.

We find it productive to let children take the lead and to place their own ideas at the center of learning and teaching mathematics in school. Children will show us what they understand and how to help them if we get to know them and watch and listen closely to what they say and do. We also want to make sure to give them opportunities to surprise us. The systems of schooling, and we ourselves, can sometimes overlook or underestimate what children are capable of. Teaching in real classrooms with real children is messy and full of tensions. We want to provide children with openings to try new things, and to struggle at times, for this too is part of learning. We want to be realistic in our expectations for young children and mindful of not pushing them too far, while also doing away with artificial limits on how they participate and learn. Children learn much more than mathematics in classrooms; they learn about who they are and who they get to be in this new world called school. It is our hope that Counting Collections can provide one of many spaces where children's ideas matter, their varied strengths are valued, and students and teachers alike feel successful.

References

Carpenter, Thomas P., Megan L. Franke, Nicholas C. Johnson, Angela C. Turrou, and Anita A. Wager. 2017. *Young Children's Mathematics: Cognitively Guided Instruction in Early Childhood Education.* Portsmouth, NH: Heinemann.

Gelman, Rochel, and C. R. Gallistel. 1986. *The Child's Understanding of Number.* 2nd ed. Cambridge, MA: Harvard University Press.

CHAPTER 7

Partnering with Families

by Carolee Koehn Hurtado and Brandon McMillan

Imagine a mom and her five-year-old son as they stroll down the sidewalk toward school, passing other homes and cars, talking along the way. "Mamá mira todos los carros en la calle" (Mom, look at all the cars on the street), the son says. The mom then asks, "¿Cuántos carros hay? ¿Podemos contar los carros? Cuenta conmigo, 1, 2, 3, . . ." (How many cars are there? Can we count the cars? Count with me, 1, 2, 3, . . .) The little boy counts the cars all the way to the school and the mom asks, "¿Cuántos hay?" (How many are there?) This is one of many examples parents share to illustrate the ways they count with their children. Many families naturally count with their children, and, as educators, we want to support them to see this work as productive and an important component of current and future mathematics learning.

Three key ideas about counting have shaped how we think about and engage with families in mathematics.

1. Counting is a key starting point for engaging families in mathematics.

We recognize that families come to school with varied education, work, and community experiences. Parents' experiences with and orientations to mathematics vary: some do not feel confident about mathematics, while others share that mathematics was one of their favorite subjects. Counting Collections and Choral Counting activities are productive starting points for engaging families because they level the playing field of experience. We've never heard anyone say they aren't good at counting—potential math anxiety is put to rest right from the start. These activities foster success and confidence and provide opportunities for participants to see themselves as mathematical thinkers.

Families count often with their young children as they begin school. They count when they play hide-and-seek, jump rope, and board games. They also count when engaged in daily routines, such as setting the table using the right number of utensils and counting money at the store. These organic, early counting experiences are a natural starting point for connecting families with Counting Collections and Choral Counting and an entry point to support them in seeing how to extend counting to support future mathematical understanding.

2. **Familiarity with counting stems from people's cultural and historical experiences.**

Counting, while developed in school, is a major part of culture and traditional commerce. To illustrate, research highlights an example of the Oksapmin people of New Guinea (Saxe 1981). The Oksapmin tribe uses a base 27 counting system predicated on using the names of twenty-seven body parts. Each language and culture has developed a counting system that supports their cultural activity. The culture's counting system is learned informally and formally through home, work, school, and community activity. Families' counting experiences may draw from a range of cultural practices and may be both similar to or different from the school experiences of their children.

Counting is also tied to language development and language development is tied to home culture and experience. In working with preschool students, we've seen students move back and forth between two languages as they count objects, demonstrating different principles of counting depending on the language. Their home and school language experiences help them to engage in the task, and both can be drawn upon to build success.

3. **Counting is useful in connecting home and school mathematics.**

Many teachers seek to build connections between home and school by having more parent engagement in the classroom, but sometimes teachers and parents are unsure how to begin this work together. Choral Counting and Counting Collections provide a means to connect families to the classroom as well as give them a way to support their children at home. Engaging families in Choral Counting and Counting Collections just as you do with students allows parents to see their children generate their own mathematical ideas and pick up and use the same ideas at home. In addition, Choral Counting and Counting Collections enable us to build on counting tasks that families already do and add to their repertoire of how to engage in counting with their children.

Families want to help their children be successful in mathematics, and they want to know what is happening in the classroom. Parents can be allies in helping students to develop their mathematical ideas. For example, they can watch for their child's one-to-one correspondence while counting or ask, "How many do you have?" after counting to reason about cardinality. As children get older, parents can begin to help them with place value and grouping by asking about how they grouped their count and how many groups constitute the number counted. The goal is not to have parents become teachers. Rather, engaging in these tasks inside and outside of school can invite families to share their own experiences and ideas as well as their child's ways of counting with school. Teachers can then learn more about what children understand and develop a two-way partnership with families for mathematical success.

Ways Educators Enact These Principles

Our goal is to create strong mathematics communities within classrooms that include families. We'll see here how teachers engage families in Counting Collections and Choral Counting activities in working one-on-one with families, collaborating with colleagues to work with many parents, and working schoolwide. We'll see teachers working with families through home visits and parent conferences, in whole-school family workshops and school math nights, in grade-level math nights, and through a counting blog. There is no one way to engage families with Choral Counting or Counting Collections, but it is critical to do so in a way that allows families to share their own expertise and understandings and that creates opportunities for families and teachers to participate together.

The Power of One: Examples from Individual Teachers

Teachers may begin to work with families in ways attuned to their particular students by interacting with families one-on-one or by hosting family workshops for their parents. Preschool and second-grade examples are highlighted.

Counting Collections: Teachers Working One-on-One with Families

Ms. Shala is a preschool teacher who works with three- to five-year-olds. As part of her preschool program, she conducts home visits with families, which affords Ms. Shala an opportunity to build rapport with her students and their families. Ms. Shala decided to make Counting Collections a focus of her home visits for the year. Connecting Counting Collections to families' lived experiences, she began by asking families to look around their homes for objects that would be interesting for children to count. She always arrived at each home equipped with her own collections but quickly realized counting became more fun when families created their own collections. Families found ways to count food, items for recycling, toys, and objects children naturally collected.

Through her home visit with Isaiah, she was able to identify his strengths and tailor learning opportunities for him. She noticed that Isaiah could recognize numerals up to 10 and count to 20. She also learned that Isaiah liked to collect rocks. She worked alongside Isaiah and his parents to count a collection of rocks. They then talked about other items that might be interesting to count. As they were getting ready for dinner, pasta seemed like a good next choice. The picture below shares Isaiah's count (see Figure 7.1). After this first home visit, Isaiah's parents excitedly shared with Ms. Shala throughout the remainder of the school year the various items he counted: fruit while shopping, Halloween candy, cereal, blocks, and pasta.

Figure 7.1
Ms. Shala and Isaiah engaging in Counting Collections at his home.

During her home visit, Ms. Shala shared a Counting Collections article with Isaiah's parents to illustrate the activity (what it could look like and its mathematical importance) and questioning strategies to encourage mathematical thinking (Schwerdtfeger and Chan 2007). Isaiah's mother shared with Ms. Shala that she learned mathematics by memorizing and executing procedures. She enjoyed reading the article because it helped her to see there are more ways to learn math and equipped her with ways to engage with her child as he created his own strategies for counting. Knowing the kinds of questions and when to ask questions significantly helped Isaiah's teacher and parents to listen to his thinking and gently nudge him to elaborate on his strategies.

Throughout the year, Ms. Shala noted that Isaiah made significant progress in counting at school. At the beginning of the year, Isaiah counted collections that contained 5 to 20 items. He progressed to recording his counting, grouped the objects in his collection, and counted to 100 by the end of the year. Isaiah's growing understanding of mathematics came from multiple counting experiences with many people in his life, both in and out of school.

While Ms. Shala, in her preschool program, had the opportunity to meet with all of her families in their home, this may not be feasible for everyone. But Ms. Shala's interactions with parents during her home visits could occur in any number of settings. For example, Ms. Montgomery, a second-grade teacher, engages parents in Counting Collections by having them come into the classroom for one-on-one meetings. As with Ms. Shala, the parents of Ms. Montgomery's students experience the activity, understand the work of young mathematicians, and develop questioning strategies to encourage more mathematical conversation at home. Another approach invites a group of parents into the classroom during mathematics time to count with the class and to discuss their noticings after the activity. This approach allows parents to see how the activity is enacted in class, engage with it themselves, and hear the conversations and questions that are posed as students count.

Combining Efforts: Collaborating with a Few Colleagues

Teachers may want to partner with colleagues to work with parents—perhaps with colleagues who share a common vision for mathematics (to engage parents in particular types of activities), with grade-level colleagues (to focus on grade-level standards or expectations), or with colleagues across a few grade levels (to illustrate how mathematical ideas develop across grades). These collaborations can happen with teachers, instructional coaches, principals, and other professional learning partners. In the following, we highlight two such efforts—one where two teachers shared a common vision for counting, and the second where a principal and mathematics instructional coach combined efforts to engage parents in their school's math goals.

Counting Collections: Two Teachers Collaborate

At Ashford Creek Elementary School, two teachers, Ms. Carney and Mr. Lopez, decided to organize a parent workshop dedicated to Counting Collections. They invited all parents from the school. The workshop involved both Spanish-speaking and English-speaking parents sitting together in table groups. Translation was available for both languages, providing an opportunity for everyone to their share thoughts with the group.

Mr. Lopez: We are going to do an activity called Counting Collections. You are going to work in partners or groups of three. One member of the group will come up to get a collection to count and a recording sheet. You and your partners are going to count all the items in the bag in a way that makes sense to you. When you are done counting, you are going to represent how you counted it on the recording sheet.
(*Parents began sorting and counting the items in their bags in different ways and setting them out on their tables. Parents shared ideas to help their group determine ways to count items and keep track of their count. After some time, parents began to write and draw how they counted their collection on their paper. See Figures 7.2 and 7.3.*)

Ms. Carney: Did you enjoy counting? Kind of fun to count, aren't they? We're going to leave your collection in the same way that you counted it on your tables. We are going to stand and do a gallery walk, where we walk around and look at the different ways people counted. One person will stay at the group and explain the way they counted. Think about what is similar and different among the ways people counted.
(*Parents circulated the room for the gallery walk, examining the different ways that groups counted their items. One group of parents walked to a table where colorful popsicle sticks were counted.*)

Lupe: Por colores . . . aquí, también por colores. (By color . . . here, also by color.)

Maria: That one is neat. Contaron cinco por cinco. (They counted by 5s.)
(*Seeing two groups of 5 with each color.*)

Karla: No diez y diez. (No by 10s.)

Lupe: No por colores. (No by colors.)

Karla: Cada grupo de palitas es diez. (Each group of sticks is 10.)

Figures 7.2 and 7.3
Parents engaging in Counting Collections together.

Maria: Ellas contaron por color después de cinco para llegar a diez. Los extra entre los colores. (They counted by color, then by 5 to get 10s. The extra they left by color.)

Maria: Como así. (Like so.) (*Pointing at sticks.*)

Lupe: ¡Buen trabajo! (Very good.)

(*After making sense of the way one group organized and counted their items, this group of parents walked to another table to identify similarities and differences. Parents continued to walk from table to table examining the ways each of the groups counted. As they finished making their way around the room, Ms. Carney brought everyone together for a discussion.*)

Ms. Carney: Let's come back together and talk about what we noticed with the whole group.

(*After the parents were back at their tables Ms. Carney continued the conversation.*)

Lucy: I noticed, out of all the groups, only one counted solely by groups of 10 and didn't organize by colors.

Ms. Carney: So, one group grouped by 10s. Why do you think they did that?

Lucy: It was just easier and fast that way.

Ms. Carney: For those that counted by color, was it easier or more difficult to add them altogether?

Lucy: We had to take time to separate by colors. Then count groups. Then count all of them, so it took longer.

Ms. Carney: One thing I'd like to share is you don't need to tell your kids how to group. Let them do this first by color, shape, or animal. Kids will develop different and more efficient ways to group, so we don't need to say first thing to do groups of 10. Let them come up with that.

This was the first time these parents participated in Counting Collections. Engaging parents with the collections, then having them do a gallery walk in which they were able to see the different ways the groups counted, allowed them to experience the activity and begin to identify the mathematics embedded within it.

While the initial evening started with 24 parents, the meeting inspired a series of mathematics-focused parent workshops. By working together, Ms. Carney and Mr. Lopez were able to build excitement around mathematics at their school with a cohort of families that consistently attended subsequent workshops throughout the school year.

Parents began seeing more mathematical opportunities around them. As they returned to other sessions, they enthusiastically shared pictures of different Counting Collections they had tried with their children. These pictures sparked an idea in the group to post pictures of Counting Collections around the school. Students were asked to count the items in the collections, find Ms. Carney to tell her how many items were in the collections, and explain how they counted. This activity created more student excitement around counting and encouraged collaboration and discussion among teachers and parents across the school. Teachers and parents mutually benefited from these workshops, ultimately creating and deepening partnerships to support their children.

Choral Counting: Efforts by a Few Educators in a School

Ms. Hayward and Ms. Padilla, the mathematics coach and principal, created a series of mathematics workshops to engage parents in instructional activities that mirrored classroom practices. In one of their workshops, parents visited a classroom, observed a choral count, and then held a meeting to discuss the activity afterward. On this day, 30 parents filled the back of the classroom to observe second-grade students during a Choral Counting task. Ms. Hayward asked students to count by 4, as she recorded their count:

4   8   12   16   20

She then asked the students to turn and talk to their partner about why they might count by 4s. Students offered ideas for items that come in packages of four, such as cookies, pencils, crayons, some families have four family members, dogs have four legs.

Ms. Hayward continued to count with the students:

4   8   12   16   20
24   28   32   36   40

Ms. Hayward: Is counting getting easier or more difficult for you? Tell your partner what you notice about your count. (*After students had some time to share their ideas with a neighbor, Ms. Hayward asked them to continue counting with her.*)

4   8   12   16   20
24   28   32   36   40
44   48   52   56   60
64   68   72   76

Ms. Hayward: What are you noticing about these numbers? I am going to give you some quiet think time. Give me a silent fist at your chest to let me know you are thinking. When you have one idea, show one finger at your chest. If you have two ideas, show me two fingers.

After waiting for some time and then scanning the room to see that students had ideas to share, Ms. Hayward gave these instructions, "Turn and tell your partner what you noticed." Students shared their noticings with their partners, and Ms. Hayward charted their thinking. Parents also whispered about their ideas to one another, and they were interested to see the patterns and hear the classroom discussion.

Following the lesson, parents met with the teacher, math coach, and principal to debrief their observations and ask questions. They were also led through their own Choral Counting task so they could experience this instructional activity as a learner. Ideas were shared in partner talk, small-group conversation, and whole-group share-outs in both English and Spanish. Parents used their primary language to help them explain their ideas and make connections to their second language. Figures 7.4–7.6 chart their noticings.

Figure 7.4

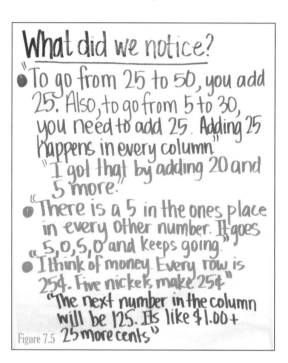

Figure 7.5

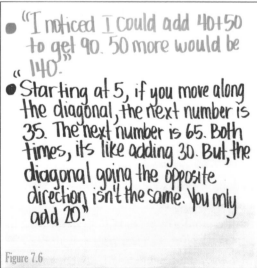

Figure 7.6

Posters of parent noticings from a choral count.

Following this task, parents were asked to identify real-life examples of skip-counting and consider ways they could encourage skip-counting with their children. They cited counting change; shopping for packaged items, such as apples or individually packaged fruit snack boxes; or planning for a birthday party (number of tables needed if each table could seat eight children). They brainstormed questions they could ask their children while they engaged in these mathematical conversations at home. During the following session, parents were excited to share their family conversations and the observations their children made while counting.

Inviting many parents into the classroom may seem daunting when trying to conduct a lesson, but in our experience, parents come away with an understanding and an appreciation of the classroom activities and how students participate. Choral Counting in the classroom with parents provides a space for parents, students, and the teacher to experience the activity together and see what it looks like to support children's developing understanding of mathematics.

Whole-School Efforts: Working Together

Whole-school efforts can communicate a schoolwide vision while allowing for grade-level-specific sessions. Participation from more teachers creates spaces for planning together, cofacilitation, and sharing of classroom practice. It also allows for larger groups of families to participate. We often see instances of whole-school family workshops in which parents and children work together to engage in mathematics. Parents learn from and with their children in these settings.

Counting Collections: Schoolwide Efforts

At Vista Elementary School, Ms. Akins, the math instructional lead teacher, sought to get all teachers involved with Counting Collections, from kindergarten through fifth grade. She created a library of collections for teachers to use, assisted in classrooms to help teachers implement Counting Collections, and facilitated ongoing discussions with teachers on refining their practice of using Counting Collections by recording student thinking and analyzing student work.

The teachers believed that an important piece to this schoolwide effort was to provide opportunities for students' families to experience Counting Collections and see the mathematical importance of these tasks. Teachers volunteered to facilitate two parent nights: one for families of students in grades K–2 and another for families of students in grades 3–5. Parents and children would engage in Counting Collections together and then learn some mathematics games they could play at home.

As students entered the classrooms with their parents, many cheered when they realized they were going to count collections. Some shared with their parents that Counting Collections was one of their favorite things to do in math. Teachers quickly realized they did not need to lead the session. Rather, they asked the students, "Please describe Counting Collections to your parent and then share what you like about Counting Collections." Children quickly took a Counting Collections bag and asked parents questions such as, "How many bears do you think are in the bag? How do you know? Let's count how many."

Teachers then asked families to engage in Counting Collections together, encouraging parents to listen to their child's thinking and not take over the thinking. Using one family's counting collection, teachers helped parents to see counting principles, such as the stable order of the sequence, one-to-one correspondence, and cardinality. Figures 7.7, 7.8, and 7.9 show a mother and her first-grade daughter engaging together in Counting Collections as well as their recordings for the two collections they counted. In these sessions, we noticed the genuine interest parents had in hearing their children's ideas for counting and recording their collection.

The second half of the evening focused on math games you can play with a deck of cards. In the two-person game of *Double Compare*, players each flip over two cards. The player who "has the most" wins the cards. Children explained to their parents how they knew who won that round. In some of the explanations, parents made connections to the counting principles they learned during the earlier session on Counting Collections. (See Figures 7.10 and 7.11.)

Figure 7.7
Parent and child engaged in Counting Collections together.

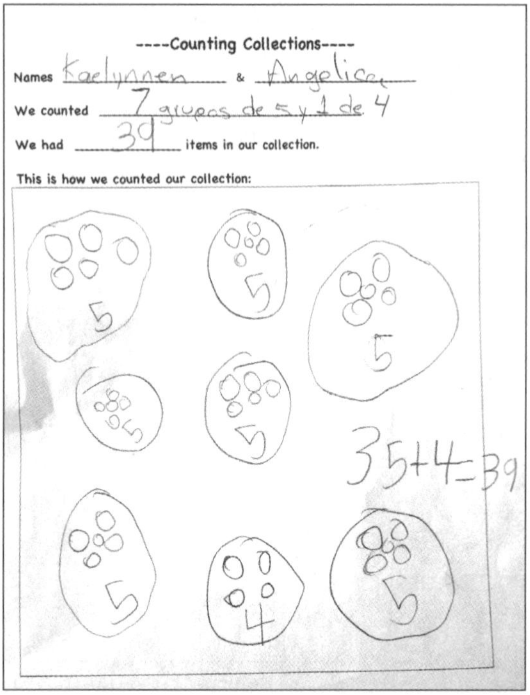

Figure 7.8
Written representations of parent and child count.

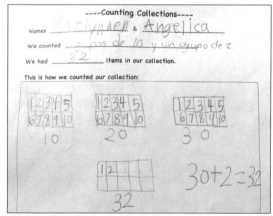

Figure 7.9
Written representations of parent and child count.

Figure 7.10
Player A

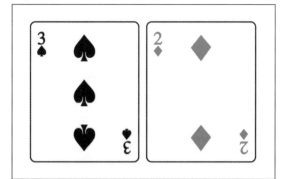

Figure 7.11
Player B

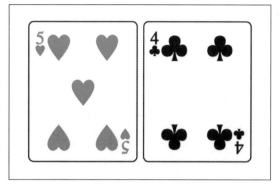

Student One: I know Player B wins because I counted 1, 2, 3, 4, 5 (*pause*), 6, 7, 8, 9. That is more than 1, 2, 3 (*pause*), 4, 5.
(*Student uses a direct modeling strategy to point to and count each object on the card using one-to-one correspondence.*)

Student Two: Player A loses because 5 is less than 9.

Parent: How do you know 5 is less than 9?

Student Two: 3, 4, 5 is less than 5, 6, 7, 8, 9.
(*Student uses a counting strategy by starting with the number on the first card, counting on the number on the next card.*)

Student Three: I see 5 for Player A. That is the same as one of the cards for Player B. Since Player B has two cards, Player B wins.
(*Student sees that the sum of the cards for Player A is equal to one of the cards for Player B. Therefore, Player B has more.*)

By focusing on Counting Collections and math games, parents were able to see mathematical ideas and make connections to these ideas across multiple contexts. Each parent engaged in and found relevance in these instructional activities. Families were encouraged to think about items in their homes they could count. Their ideas included grapes, stairs, shoes, pencils, coins, the number of fingers in one's family, and things they saw while walking in the neighborhood, such as leaves and rocks. Families were also given decks of cards to take home.

As the year progressed, all teachers implemented Counting Collections in their classrooms. The school reported that the work with parents allowed teachers to assign different kinds of homework: students could now do Counting Collections at home with items that were of interest to them. Ms. Akins is now considering expanding the school counting collection library to include collections that students can check out for counting at home.

At Vista Elementary School, math nights had been a practice used by the staff to develop excitement with mathematics. This had previously occurred with math games for parents to play with their children. The inclusion of Counting Collections and Choral Counting brought a new excitement to the school, providing another connection between school and home. Vista noticed a marked increase in the number of parents attending future sessions.

Choral Counting: Schoolwide Efforts

Marine Elementary School began implementing more number sense and reasoning activities with their students. Parents reported to teachers that math homework was looking different: both in terms of the amount assigned (fewer problems) and the type of work students were being asked to complete (moving from textbook problems and worksheets to number sense and problem-solving activities). Teachers and the principal thought it would be advantageous to host a parent night to introduce parents to the school's instructional goals and methodology, while engaging parents in firsthand experiences with classroom mathematical activities.

The school was pleasantly surprised to have 200 parents and children attend the event, which started in the cafeteria with parents and children together. In the Choral Counting task, Ms. Recinos asked the group to count by 6s while she charted the numbers they counted. Families counted aloud together. Pausing at 60, Ms. Recinos, asked families to stop and think about the next three numbers they would say when they continued to count. She then asked them to make a conjecture, "Do you think we will land on 100 when we continue to count? Share with your neighbor how you know."

After the group counted to 132 (it was a goal to count beyond 100!), Ms. Recinos asked them to stop counting and quietly think about what they noticed in the charted count. At the tables, the count was provided to each family as a handout along with colored pencils.

6	12	18	24	30
36	42	48	54	60
66	72	78	84	90
96	102	108	114	120
126	132			

The cafeteria was abuzz with children and adults enthusiastically sharing their findings. Parents seemed as excited to share as their children. This experience allowed school educators to illustrate the mathematical thinking they were striving for in the classroom. Following the choral count, families rotated between three other classrooms in smaller groups to experience problem solving using word problems, math games they could play at home, and Counting Collections. Two teachers paired together to facilitate each classroom. For each rotation, the teacher pair facilitated the same 15- to 20-minute activity with a different group of parents. This structure allowed for schoolwide family workshops, with each teacher co-responsible for a small portion of the evening.

Connecting with Families Through a Math Wall and Math Blog

Teachers at Bellevue Elementary collectively decided to engage their students in Counting Collections in all grades, K–5. To further these efforts, the math committee aimed to make this work visible to the children, fellow teachers at the site, families of their children, and school visitors. They hoped to highlight the complexity of students' mathematical thinking, to encourage colleagues to learn from one another, and to share instructional practice with families of their community.

Counting Collections had become an instructional practice in every classroom and was an integral part of the school's mathematics focus. The math committee sought to unify the efforts around Counting Collections through the creation of a math wall to display student work and a math blog for parents. Mr. Sagun, a teacher on the math committee, volunteered to collect photos and student work from every teacher to make their math focus explicit for parents and visitors.

As Mr. Sagun worked alongside teachers and visited classrooms, he took on the task of capturing and documenting the range of student thinking and the mathematical importance of Counting Collections, with the goal of sharing this with an audience that may not know why they, as a school community, were focusing on counting. He wanted to make the mathematics visible and help others see the value in this work. Each picture of student work included the students' reasoning and an explanation of the important mathematical concepts evident in the work.

Displaying this counting work in the main hallway of the school allowed students, parents, visitors, and other teachers to see the counting experiences from different classes and the ways the mathematical ideas built across the grades. Students in the lower grades often took tours around the school to interact with the math wall. They were intrigued to see photos of their older peers' Counting Collections. By looking at larger collections, they noticed many ways to organize and group items to make the task of counting easier. When older students looked at these same students' groupings, teachers challenged them to write one number sentence that matched how that group of students counted their collection. The displayed student work allowed for interactions and engagement in other's ideas, thus supporting communication and mathematical thinking. (See Figure 7.12.)

Families noticed the development of mathematical thinking across grade levels and often stopped to see the different collections. As parents looked at the math wall more, questions about the mathematics from counting began to surface. In response to these questions, Bellevue Elementary hosted days to welcome parents into classrooms during counting activities and to engage together with the work on the math wall. The teachers paid particular attention to parents' questions about math, counting, and the frequency of Counting Collections. Some parents wondered why their children were counting, why older children were still counting, and why so much time was given to what some people consider a basic skill.

To create a window into classroom practice and to share more detail around their students' counting work, the math committee decided to create a blog to share with parents. They realized it was important to show the mathematical

Figure 7.12
Displaying Counting
Collections on the
math wall.

thinking that comes from engaging in counting and to demonstrate the complexity of that thinking as students get older. The school mathematics blog was similar to the math wall in that teachers throughout the school posted pictures of collections by students and explanations of the way items were counted. The blog served as a way to reach more family members as parents could access the blog at any time of day.

The math wall and blog from Bellevue Elementary demonstrate ways to engage with parents around counting other than in person. By making the scenes of the classroom evident and available, families and other teachers felt connected to what was going on in classrooms. The display provided talking points for families when they shared with the teacher what they noticed as they counted at home. Bellevue also found that the math wall and blog enabled teachers to share their practice with one another and to have instructional conversations with colleagues of similar and different grades.

Why Engage Families in Counting Collections and Choral Counting?

Counting Collections is an instructional activity that travels nicely between school and home; children can naturally engage in Counting Collections of the abundant objects in their environment. Choral Counting might serve a different purpose. By engaging parents in the activity of Choral Counting, families can see the thinking students are engaged in during class and consider times in their day when they can engage their children in counting. The take-away here is not for parents to create Choral Counting tasks but, rather, for parents to see how informal interactions could support their children's number sense. In both Counting Collections and Choral Counting, our hope is to create spaces for families and educators to engage in two-way dialogue around supporting children in mathematics: parents can share ways they interact with their children, and schools can invite families into their efforts.

Mathematical Content Goals

We have found Counting Collections and Choral Counting to be nonthreatening ways to engage families in a multitude of mathematical ideas. For instance, through Counting Collections with small quantities, parents begin to notice the importance of early counting principles. As they count larger collections, we see parents (just as children would) begin to naturally group objects to make counting easier. Facilitators can use these natural groupings both in counting large quantities and in counting packages to highlight important mathematical ideas such as multiple groups (multiplication), place value, use of parentheses, order of operations, and the fundamental mathematical properties such as the commutative property, associative property, and the distributive property of multiplication over addition. Some facilitators have also used Counting Collections to invite children and parents into ideas with fractions and exponents.

Choral Counting tasks encourage parents to count by whole numbers, fractions or decimals. Through careful recording by the facilitator, parents can look for number relations, make conjectures, and provide justification as they articulate what they see. Parents often build on one another's ideas as they share their own noticings in ways that allow for an extension of the mathematics. Parents get a chance to work on making their informal ideas formal and see how these counting activities support the development of many sophisticated mathematical ideas.

Getting Started

We have shared here several ways educators have counted with families, along with their particular goals for these endeavors. Our intention was to provide a diversity of examples that spark ideas for readers as they think about their own efforts to engage families in their children's mathematics.

In starting or enhancing math parent engagement practices at your school, we encourage you to consider and talk with colleagues about these questions.

1. What details in the vignettes support families' engagement in counting? Be sure to cite examples, and make explicit your assumptions.
2. Which approach and details make sense in terms of your own situation?
3. How does your approach or planned approach make use of families' existing counting practices?

Planning

After reflecting on current practices, begin planning some work that you may want to do at your school or district. In thinking about hosting or facilitating family mathematics sessions, you may want to consider your facilitation team, audience, and resources. For instance:

•   Will you invite families from your class only, from your grade level, or everyone in your school?
•   Would you find it helpful to get started by partnering with one or more colleagues, either as a planning partner or a cofacilitator?

- Do you want to engage parents only or parents with children? You may find you structure the event differently based on the participants you expect to attend.
- Elicit feedback from parents both before and after workshops to help you plan for future events. Schools often have the best intentions of offering parent workshops yet unilaterally make decisions without parent input. Parents have many ideas and are often willing to share their ideas with schools. Feedback can be helpful to find out what parents are interested in and what days and times work best for the community.
- What resources might parents be able to take with them to support their continued engagement? It's a bonus if parents have access to resources, such as a library of Counting Collections they can check out for home use.

In planning for your event, participation and engagement are important.

Family Participation: How might you encourage parents to attend these workshops? Are there ways you can partner with other groups on campus to help you reach out to parents to make personal invitations to attend? Some teachers like to hand out flyers during student pick-up after school or visit other meetings on campus. We suggest advertising workshops in a fun, nonthreatening way to minimize the fear of math and to illustrate a safe, fun environment. Food and childcare at parent workshops is always helpful, too.

Participant Engagement: How will you encourage parents to engage in your session? Consider translating written information and verbal contributions into languages that your families speak or use grouping strategies so that all participants can listen to one another's ideas and share their own ideas. These workshops will be much more interesting for both you and your participants if everyone has a chance to share their ideas.

Working with families has helped us more substantially realize their value.

1. Families are an important, but often underused asset to the school for both support and academic learning.
2. Counting and doing mathematics with families empower them within the school community and at home to make sense of what their children are learning in school and to see how to support their own children both in and out of school.
3. Parent engagement should be an opportunity for two-way communication between school and home. Families can learn from schools and schools can learn from families.

Traditional notions of families in schools often operate from involvement models, where schools invite parents to engage in activities such as back-to-school nights, chaperoning field trips, and volunteering to prepare materials. While these types of activities are important, they are not sufficient for providing families with opportunities to share their family practices or to learn more about instructional goals and activities. By engaging families in spaces that position them as knowledgeable contributors, such as some of the examples we have shared, schools can learn how families engage their children in counting, and parents can learn from teachers. This mutual learning further supports children's academic learning, at school and at home.

References

Saxe, Geoffrey B. 1981. "Body Parts as Numerals: A Developmental Analysis of Numeration Among the Oksapmin in Papua New Guinea." *Child Development* 52 (1): 306–316.

Schwerdtfeger, Julie Kern, and Chan, Angela. 2007. "Counting Collections." *Teaching Children Mathematics* 13 (7): 356–361.

CHAPTER 8

Conclusion

by Megan L. Franke, Elham Kazemi, and Angela Chan Turrou

We began this book with an invitation for you to consider the mathematics you can open up for your students by incorporating two rather simple activities into your instruction. We hope you have seen the power of regular opportunities for students to count across the elementary grades and the joyful curiosities they can provoke in your classroom.

We see Counting Collections and Choral Counting as activities that can create opportunities for conversations between families and schools and do so in ways that challenge our understandings and assumptions about our students. We can counter the practices in schools that encourage us to sort students by ability or to narrowly define mathematics as a discipline in which only a few can experience success. We intentionally included chapters on working with our youngest learners and working with families because we believe that how educators and families work together in partnership has everything to do with realizing our goals for equitable learning opportunities for students. We find this work challenging and offer an example to help make explicit how attending to students and their ideas and using counting activities together can open up space for student learning.

Marquis's Story

Marquis was a fourth-grader in Lynn Simpson's classroom when the school began a deliberate effort to work together to change the culture of the school toward more collaborative, meaningful, and joyful learning opportunities for both students and teachers. The school was located in a low-income neighborhood serving a beautifully rich and diverse group of students—recent refugees and immigrants from East Africa, Asian American students, Latina/o students, African American students, and small populations of Native American and White students. The school had not been performing well, and the staff had the chance to start moving in a new direction. Ms. Simpson recounted how she put together what she was learning about children's thinking with her commitments to support her students and families.

Ms. Simpson learned early on in the year that Marquis was feeling very discouraged about his own abilities in math. He told her that he only liked math a little bit. He didn't think other students could learn from his strategies even though he did enjoy sharing them during class. She recounted the conversation she had with Marquis's mom at a parent/teacher conference.

> So, in November when Marquis's mom came in for a conference, she shared with me, and, it wasn't a surprise, that he was really not enjoying math. He had told his Mom that he wanted to go into special education for math because he didn't get it.

Ms. Simpson had observed that, while Marquis understood the relationships in word problems, he became discouraged sometimes when working with large numbers because he was counting by ones most of the time. She had developed some insight into what was hard for Marquis as she watched him solve several problems. For example, take a look at what happened when he tried to solve the problem: *Zoey had 8 packs of pencils. There are 12 pencils in each pack. How many pencils does she have?* He drew the 8 packs of pencils and drew 12 pencils in each. This nicely showed that he understood the mathematical relationships in the problem. For his answer, he wrote 95, although at first, he had written 59 and crossed it out because he had reversed the numerals. Watching him count was invaluable for Ms. Simpson as she puzzled through what was going on for Marquis. When she asked him how he counted the total, he said that he knew that 12 plus 12 was 24 and then from there he had counted by 1s. At 69, he paused, trying to think of the number that came next and said 70. At 79, he paused again and said 90. Some of the tallies are close together so missing a couple along the way got him to his answer of 95. This was really interesting. As a fourth grader, Marquis would be working with big numbers so noticing these counting errors was very helpful. (See Figure 8.1.)

It was becoming clearer that Marquis would really benefit from counting work. When he tried another problem, *Ahmed has 246 pieces of candy. He wants to put 10 candies in each box. How many boxes will he need? How many candies will be left over?* he said, "That means I have to draw 246 dots! I wonder if I can

Figure 8.1
Marquis's work for solving the multiplication problem about packs of pencils.

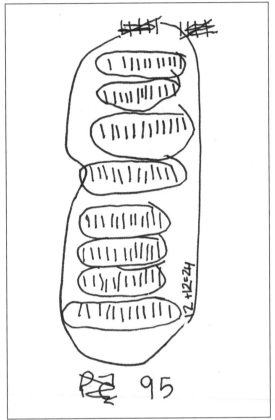

do it another way. Usually a kid would draw dots or tally marks if the number isn't big. I have done this before with easier numbers. I'm not sure I know how to start." Numbers that should not have been overwhelming for Marquis were. These close observations of Marquis at work were important to better understand what he was making sense of and what we needed to work on. No wonder he felt discouraged about math.

Because Ms. Simpson was paying close attention to how Marquis was feeling and what he was doing and thinking about as he solved problems, she acted on some hunches that she felt would help him. Let's hear how she continued to recount what came of the interaction with Marquis's mother at the conference.

And so we had just done all the Counting Collections stuff and so I taught her how to do Counting Collections. And I told her, "He doesn't have to do any of the other assigned homework if you will commit to doing this with him every night. Have him practice—make 10, make 10 plus a number, and doing counts, grouping into 10s, grouping into 100s—and practice representing it." And I taught her how to do it. She went home and she has been doing that. She has him counting beans or rubber bands or whatever it is. And so two and a half weeks after he started doing that, there was a problem he was working on. It involved the distributive property, where you had to figure out two multiplication problems and then add them together. He had done the first one and gotten an answer of 120 and he did the second one and got 28. And I said, "What's your next step?" He said, "Well, 120 and 28, that's 148." He could do that in his head. So that was pretty exciting. And then just this week, we were talking about why does it work when you're trying to figure out 6 × 40, to think about 6 × 4. So he wrote down 6 × 4 = 24, because he knew that fact, and then underneath it he put 6 × 40 = 240. I said, "How did you know that?" He explained it in front of the class on the overhead. He said, "Well, I knew that 40 was the tenth multiple of 4. So 240 has to be the tenth multiple of 24." My jaw dropped, and my eyes welled up a little bit with tears. I was just so excited. And some kids asked him to repeat it. And he repeated it just as fluently as he had done the first time. He was really under-standing the concept that we are working on right now. Understanding what happens when you multiply a number by a multiple of 10.

   So I talked to his mother last night. She said, "Yes, absolutely he's feeling a lot better about math. He's doing the homework." He started doing home-work again even though he wasn't required to because he felt that he could do it. He is much happier, and he is more confident, raising his hands more, par-ticipating. He's been counting for two months, every night. He just needs his hands on things, counting them to construct place value and grouping and how to think about numbers. He just didn't have enough experience.

By the end of the year, the problem that had vexed him at the beginning of the year was no longer a challenge. His classwork, including his work with Counting Collections, had helped him develop stronger understandings about the structure of number. We asked him in the spring to share how he would solve the problem: *Ahmed has 246 pieces of candy. He wants to put 10 candies in each box. How many boxes will he need? How many candies will be left over?* He confidently stated, "There are twenty 10s in 200, four more 10s in 40, and 6 left over. That makes 24 full boxes of candy." (See Figure 8.2.)

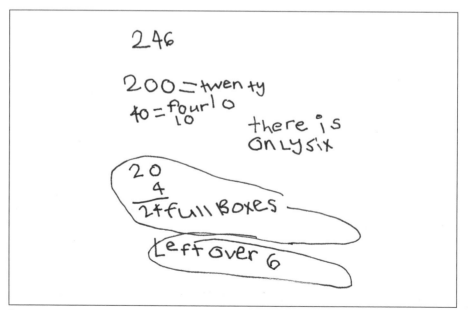

Figure 8.2
Marquis's work showing his growth in understanding the structure of number.

Marquis showed tremendous growth in his fourth-grade year and left feeling as though learning mathematics was about his ideas. The partnership between his teacher and his mother also showed the power of attending to students and learning what is hard for them instead of just labeling them as struggling learners. When students share their thinking with us, they help us learn a lot about what makes sense and what doesn't. In Marquis's case, the work he did with counting was transformational in how he understood the structure of number and his confidence in his own capabilities.

Connections Between Choral Counting and Counting Collections

We imagine you're thinking about how to use these activities in your classroom. You are probably thinking about how you might integrate them into your normal routines. One thing we'd like to help you imagine is how Choral Counting and Counting Collections complement each other.

In our work with teachers and students, we have discovered that Choral Counting and Counting Collections work together in important ways. The activities work to support the coordination of important aspects of number, the verbal (how you say a number, "three"), quantitative (the amount), and symbolic notation (how you write the number 3). Choral Counting gives young students opportunities to work on how to say the number—integers, fractions, and decimals—and see the number in its written form. As teachers make posters/anchor charts, they can leave these up in their classrooms so students can continue to study how to write particular numbers. Students can refer to these charts as they record their collections when engaging in Counting Collections activities.

Choral Counting can also help students feel confident about their ability to count by different increments—2s, 10s, 15s, 25s—which can support them to choose a more efficient way of counting their collections. For example, a teacher shared that, in her first-grade classroom, after a few weeks of engaging in Counting Collections, she noticed that many students were counting their collections by ones. The teacher was hoping more students would start to group their collections by 5s or 10s. So she had a mathematical goal of supporting students to work on counting by 5s and 10s, as well as see patterns in their counts.

The teacher planned a few choral counts by 5s and 10s, in order to support students to be ready to count their collections by groups. She began doing these counts immediately before sending students off to count their collections. The teacher even made a suggestion to the students: "Some of you were thinking about grouping by 10s. Maybe this chart will help you count your collection today." She referred to the patterns the students noticed in the choral count when the students started to group by 5s or 10s, in order to help them to make connections between the two activities.

In the upper grades, when Mr. Peterson's students began counting large collections of more than 2,000 items, they were looking for ways to keep track of their groups. Many students were counting by 50, so Mr. Peterson planned a count by 50 and invited students to think about how the count related to their collection.

Choral Counting or Counting Collections can also provide the structure to investigate questions students generate about number. A student's idea such as, "I think ten thousand is one million two hundreds maybe?" could launch an interesting follow-up investigation for the whole class: how many 200s *do* fit inside of 10,000? A count by 200 or work with a collection could help answer this question. Opportunities like this may naturally emerge in your counting work together. Also, as you gain familiarity with Choral Counting and your students, you can become more strategic in your selection of choral counts.

The representations created by Choral Counting and Counting Collections can be useful resources for students' problem-solving. For example, Ms. Moe's fourth graders generated useful strategies for counting by thirds and finding equivalent fractions. Later in the day when they were working on fraction word problems, some students referred to their choral count as a way to solve some of the problems.

Counting and Community Connections

Counting is not just a school task. Sending students out into the community to interview people who use counting as part of their job can be a fruitful way for them to recognize mathematics in everyday activities and work. You might consider having students, supervised and with adult support, ask a community worker about what and how they count, what systems or tools help them, what counting challenges they face, and how accuracy impacts their work. Through community interviews, students have learned about the surprisingly complex challenges faced by adults who count for their work, including flight attendants, knitters, cashiers, restaurant managers, dry cleaners, childcare workers, booksellers, blood bank workers, and many more. Here are some insights students gained from these community counting interviews:

"Counting is very important to music. My dad counts bars, beats per minute (BPM), and measures. He uses a tool called a metronome to count the BPM. I never realized there was a connection between math and music." —Donovan R.

"The main issue [with counting at Trader Joe's] would be distractions. When they are putting merchandise out on the shelves they have to count, but sometimes a customer asks for help, and they have to stop what they are doing. There are times when they have to start counting all over again." —Sofia R.

"Ashley has 5 babies in her day care. She counts how many bottles of milk she has to give to the babies. She uses measuring bottles to count the ounces of milk the babies drink. She uses a daily sheet to record and keep track of how many hours the babies sleep, how much they eat, and how much diapers they use." —Kal C.

"I met Ms. Mendoza who works as an attractions hostess at Disneyland. She counts people that want to go on the rides. At Pirates . . . 23 people fit in each boat. If the boat is too heavy, it will sink lower and will take longer to get through the ride because the boat is going too slow. Overfilling the boat also creates safety issues and makes the wait for the line longer." —Genevieve S.

"I interviewed my Uncle Papa. He is a flight attendant on American Airlines. He said precision is necessary when dealing with the coach section of the aircraft because food and alcohol must be charged and accounted for. Also when counting passengers [he] must come to a precise number." —Beija S.

"I interviewed Matthew who is the owner of Mar Vista Cleaners. He talked about how he needs to count four things to run that type of business: the clothes that people give him, the pieces that he sends to the laundry, the money people pay him, and the supplies he needs to run the business. He always gets an exact number because he confirms the number of clothes with the customer and puts the invoices in alphabetical order." —William B.

These interviews provided context for conversations about accuracy, tools, and efficiency, and gave the class a way to relate their work as counters in the classroom with people who count in important ways in their communities too. You will innovate your own ways to connect your students with real-world mathematics—there is plenty of counting going on in the world around us. There are imperfect or problematic systems to which our elementary students could offer thoughtful and inventive solutions.

Advice from Teachers

We asked teachers to share with us advice they would give to others beginning to work with Choral Counting and Counting Collections. We end our book with their voices and encourage you to get connected with us on Twitter through these hashtags, #countingcollections and #choralcounting.

> *Just try it! Start out simple and then continue to build and grow with your students! You will see how students are engaged and growing their brains! It may seem chaotic to do Counting Collections at first, but be brave, it is worth the organized chaos! My suggestion is find a buddy or fellow teacher to try it out as well. Plan together and then debrief after you have both tried it so you can learn from what worked and what you need to revise.*
>
> —*Hannah Yazzolino, teacher*

> *It may be messy and confusing in the beginning, but stick with it. Your students' thinking and discussions will help guide you.*
>
> —*Kimberly Buck, teacher*

> *Try it but don't give up! It is the best, seemingly "chaotic" learning experience for both students and teacher. You have to give yourself time to learn, reflect, and revise as you dive into these activities. If you can be patient with yourself and your students, you won't regret it.*
>
> —*Atoosa Abascal, coach*

> *Counting Collections encourages students to think about our base 10 number system in an organic fashion. Teachers aren't telling students to group by tens but instead are asking questions like, "How else can you count them?" so that students can reach their own conclusions about groupings that might create more efficiency for them. This provides a sense of ownership and agency that typical textbook exercises lack.*
>
> —*Andrew Jenkins, principal*

Math isn't just about memorizing facts or coming up with strategies to solve problems. It's about listening, sharing, questioning, and adding to each other's mathematical ideas. Choral Counting is a great platform for kids to have those conversations with each other. The math talk that happens during this activity allows students to agree and respectfully disagree with their peers, question each other's thinking, or offer a different perspective to the group. It encourages kids to think critically and to learn to defend their own ideas.

—*Gia Meade, teacher*

These activities help students think deeply about number sense and builds upon what they already know. The hardest part is keeping their excitement contained! They love noticing patterns when Choral Counting and utilizing that knowledge to make predictions about future numbers. They also thoroughly enjoy Counting Collections, oftentimes bringing in collections they have done at home after being inspired in the classroom.

—*Monica Acosta, teacher*

It's a funny thing about counting. Many believe that it is a very simple process and often think that the end goal of that learning is rote counting. It's as easy as 1, 2, 3, right? Nope. It is very complex and requires students to engage in the work of counting regularly. When I engage students in Counting Collections, I see opportunities for students to refine their counting practice, work collaboratively with a counting partner to build social and math communication skills. I also have the grand opportunity as the teacher to observe my students while they count to determine where they are in their learning and where to guide them next.

—*Jamie Garner, teacher*

Go ahead! Be curious. Get messy. Delight in this work with your students, families, and communities. Play.

Counting Collections Recording Sheets

Appendix 1.1   Counting Collections Recording Sheet

Name _____ Date _____

Bag _____

How many items were there?_____

Show how you counted.

Appendix 1.2   Adding Collections

Group 1:	Group 2:

Total:

Show how you know your total:

Appendix 1.3   Counting Collections: Recording Sheets with Reflection

Name _____ Date _____

Bag _____

How many items were there? _____

Show how you counted.

Reflection

One thing I learned from my partner _____

_____

My goal next time we do Counting Collections is to _____

_____

Appendix 1.4   Counting Collections: How Many More?

Name _____ Date _____

1. Record the amount you counted _____

2. Draw a representation of your collection:

3. How many more objects will you need to have _____?

4. Show how you figured out how many more.

Appendix 1.5   Counting Collections: How Many More to 100?

Name _____ Date _____

Show a representation of your collection here:

How many more of your collection would you need to have 100?

Choral Counting Planning Templates

Version 1   Choral Counting Planning Template

Count by _____ , starting at _____ , going up / down.

Anticipated Student Strategies	Record of Count and Patterns
Planned Pauses	

Anticipated student noticing and responses/extension questions

Version 2   Choral Counting Planning Template

Choral Count: _____

```
┌─────────────────────────────────────────────────────────┐
│                                                           │
│   Choral Count Representation on Board                    │
│                                                           │
│                                                           │
│                                                           │
│                                                           │
│                                                           │
│                                                           │
│                                                           │
│                                                           │
│                                                           │
│                                                           │
│                                                           │
└─────────────────────────────────────────────────────────┘
```

Anticipated Questions, Noticings, Ideas to Pursue During Count

Where to Find More Examples of Choral Counting and Counting Collections

Learn About Number Systems in Many Cultures

http://www.languagesandnumbers.com

Access Resources to Support Teacher Learning of Counting Collections and Choral Counting

tedd.org/

Twitter Hashtags

#countingcollections
#choralcounting
#tmwyk (talk math with your kids)

Articles and Books

Schwerdtfeger, Julie Kern, and Angela Chan. 2007. "Counting Collections." *Teaching Children Mathematics* 13 (7): 356–361.

Turrou, Angela Chan, Megan L. Franke, and Nicholas Johnson. 2017. "Choral Counting." *Teaching Children Mathematics* 24 (2): 129–135.

Zager, Tracy. 2017. *Becoming the Math Teacher You Wish You'd Had: Ideas and Strategies from Vibrant Classrooms.* Portland, ME: Stenhouse. See Chapter 10.

Videos

Counting Collections—Kindergarten

https://www.teachingchannel.org/videos/skip-counting-with-kindergarteners
https://www.teachingchannel.org/videos/visualizing-number-combinations

Choral Counting and Counting Collections—Grade 1

https://www.teachingchannel.org/videos/counting-by-ten-lesson

Choral Counting—Grade 1

https://www.teachingchannel.org/blog/2017/06/23/choral-counting-number-routine/

Choral Counting—Grade 3

https://www.teachingchannel.org/videos/teaching-number-patterns

Counting Collections—Grade 3

https://www.teachingchannel.org/videos/counting-collections-lesson

Blog Posts Regarding Counting Collections

http://tjzager.com/2015/12/10/counting-circles-variant-tens-and-ones/
http://tjzager.com/2014/09/05/the-structure-of-popovers/
http://tjzager.com/2015/11/22/the-steep-part-of-the-learning-curve/
http://exit10a.blogspot.com/2015/12/22-30-50-100.html
https://thelearningkaleidoscope.wordpress.com/2015/11/03/counting-realia/
http://blogs.sd38.bc.ca/sd38mathandscience/2016/10/18/introducing-counting-collections-in-kindergarten/

Counting Collections in Special Education Settings

https://mathmindsblog.wordpress.com/2016/01/24/counting-is-complex/
https://mathmindsblog.wordpress.com/2016/02/05/obsessed-with-counting-collections/
https://mathmindsblog.wordpress.com/2016/02/08/counting-collections-extension/

Counting Collections with Older Students

http://www.nctm.org/Publications/Teaching-Children-Mathematics/Blog/Counting_-Why-is-it-Important-and-How-Do-We-Support-Children_-Part-1/

http://www.theletteredclassroom.com/2016/03/counting-collections.html
http://mathforlove.com/lesson/counting-collections/

Blog Posts Regarding Choral Counting

https://davidwees.com/content/choral-counting/
http://exit10a.blogspot.com/2016/02/a-post-about-counting-circles.html
http://www.nctm.org/Publications/Teaching-Children-
  Mathematics/Blog/Counting-Activities-to-Try-with-Primary-Students/
https://bstockus.wordpress.com/tag/choral-counting/
https://kgmathminds.com/2017/06/18/choral-count-trusting-patterns/
http://missmcguirencs.blogspot.com/2011/11/choral-counting.html
http://blog.graceachen.com/2015/05/choral-counting-language-question.html
https://cjsharpe.expressions.syr.edu/2018/03/16/using-choral-counts-for-
  exploring-fraction-relationships/
https://mathontheedge.com/2017/11/13/decimals-backwards-slashes-and-
  giggling-in-math-class/

Blog Posts Regarding Counting Conversations at Home

https://aofradkin.wordpress.com/2015/07/07/counting-geese/
https://talkingmathwithkids.com/2013/08/17/armholes/

Index